ART
& SOUL,
RELOADED

ALSO BY PAM GROUT

BOOKS

*Thank & Grow Rich:
A 30-day Experiment in Shameless
Gratitude and Unabashed Joy*
(also available as an audiobook)*

*E-Cubed: Nine More
Energy Experiments That
Prove Manifesting Magic and
Miracles Is Your Full-Time Gig*
(also available as an audiobook)*

*E-Squared: Nine Do-It-Yourself
Energy Experiments That Prove Your
Thoughts Create Your Reality*
(also available as an audiobook)*

*Jumpstart Your Metabolism:
How to Lose Weight by
Changing the Way You Breathe*

*Living Big: Embrace Your Passion
and Leap into an Extraordinary Life*
(also available as an audiobook)

*Kansas Curiosities: Quirky
Characters, Roadside Oddities
& Other Offbeat Stuff*

*Colorado Curiosities: Quirky
Characters, Roadside Oddities
& Other Offbeat Stuff*

*Girlfriend Getaways:
You Go Girl! And I'll Go, Too*

*You Know You're in Kansas
When . . . : 101 Quintessential
Places, People, Events, Customs, Lingo,
and Eats of the Sunflower State*

*Recycle This Book:
And 72 1/2 Even Better Ways
to Save "Yo Momma" Earth*

*God Doesn't Have Bad Hair Days:
Ten Spiritual Experiments That
Will Bring More Abundance, Joy,
and Love to Your Life*

*The 100 Best Vacations
to Enrich Your Life*

*The 100 Best Worldwide
Vacations to Enrich Your Life*

*The 100 Best Volunteer
Vacations to Enrich Your Life*

CARD DECK

*The Oracle of E: A 52-Card Deck and
Guidebook to Manifest Your Dreams*
(with Colette Baron-Reid)*

* Available from Hay House
Please visit:

Hay House UK: www.hayhouse.co.uk
Hay House USA: www.hayhouse.com®
Hay House Australia: www.hayhouse.com.au
Hay House South Africa: www.hayhouse.co.za
Hay House India: www.hayhouse.co.in

ART & SOUL, RELOADED

A YEARLONG APPRENTICESHIP FOR
SUMMONING THE MUSES AND RECLAIMING YOUR
BOLD, AUDACIOUS CREATIVE SIDE

PAM GROUT

HAY HOUSE

Carlsbad, California • New York City • London
Sydney • Johannesburg • Vancouver • New Delhi

First published and distributed in the United Kingdom by:
Hay House UK Ltd, Astley House, 33 Notting Hill Gate, London W11 3JQ
Tel: +44 (0)20 3675 2450; Fax: +44 (0)20 3675 2451; www.hayhouse.co.uk

Published and distributed in the United States of America by:
Hay House Inc., PO Box 5100, Carlsbad, CA 92018-5100
Tel: (1) 760 431 7695 or (800) 654 5126
Fax: (1) 760 431 6948 or (800) 650 5115; www.hayhouse.com

Published and distributed in Australia by:
Hay House Australia Ltd, 18/36 Ralph St, Alexandria NSW 2015
Tel: (61) 2 9669 4299; Fax: (61) 2 9669 4144; www.hayhouse.com.au

Published and distributed in the Republic of South Africa by:
Hay House SA (Pty) Ltd, PO Box 990, Witkoppen 2068
info@hayhouse.co.za; www.hayhouse.co.za

Published and distributed in India by:
Hay House Publishers India, Muskaan Complex, Plot No.3, B-2,
Vasant Kunj, New Delhi 110 070
Tel: (91) 11 4176 1620; Fax: (91) 11 4176 1630; www.hayhouse.co.in

Distributed in Canada by:
Raincoast Books, 2440 Viking Way, Richmond, B.C. V6V 1N2
Tel: (1) 604 448 7100; Fax: (1) 604 270 7161; www.raincoast.com

A catalogue record for this book is available from the British Library.

First edition published as *Art and Soul: 156 Ways to Free Your Creative Spirit*, ISBN: 978-0-7407-0482-6

ISBN: 978-1-78180-622-7

Printed and bound by CPI Group (UK) Ltd, Croydon, CR0 4YY

*This one's for Taz, the
most creative person I know*

CONTENTS

SECTION 2: Tapping the Divine

SECTION 3: *Kill Bill*

SECTION 4: Generating Creative Capital (or, Why You Should Tell Netflix Where to Go)

SECTION 5: Uplifting the World

*"What if imagination and art
are not frosting at all, but the
fountainhead of human experience?"*

— ROLLO MAY, EXISTENTIAL PSYCHOLOGIST

❦ PREFACE ❦

"Say yes if you're an artist. Say yes if you've known it from the beginning of time."

— RUMI, 13TH-CENTURY PERSIAN POET

I wrote this book 18 years ago. Until *E-Squared*, the international bestseller that changed my life, it was by far my personal favorite. It sprang out of my own creative questions, my own artistic struggle. It was driven by my desire to connect to the bigger thing that, as far as I could tell, had somehow appointed me to be a writer, had for some reason gifted me with the skill set to do this job.

I discovered in my career as a writer that when I asked for help from the muses, from the universe, from God, my writing flowed more smoothly. I found my creativity worked best when I set aside my own crazy voices and agreed to show up and act as a satellite dish.

Creativity, it seems, has much in common with spirituality and may, in fact, be the same thing.

When I surrendered to the bigger thing, all sorts of unexpected miracles were orchestrated on my behalf. New writing gigs, the perfect quote, the exact resource I needed showed up in surprising and mysterious ways.

Even so, the first incarnation of *E-Squared* (it originally debuted as *God Doesn't Have Bad Hair Days*) and the 18-year-old version of this book met the same fate. They went out of print not long after making their respective debuts. Ironically, these personal favorites were the only 2 of my 18 books to do so.

I revived *Hair Days* four years ago, turned it into *E-Squared*, and, well, it finally found its audience. I trust this book will, too.

I guess what I'm trying to say is: I still love this book. I believe it has a timeless message. I hope you'll agree.

✎ INTRODUCTION ৫

"I used to be dangerous. I don't know what happened."

— JUDITH MOORE, FROM THE MOVIE
LIVING OUT LOUD

All my life, I've been a closet bohemian. Even though I grew up in a small Kansas town, was a minister's daughter, a straight-A student, and a Goody Two-shoes, I always longed to live big, be outrageous.

Outside, I was Pam Grout, junior achiever. But inside, I have always been Isadora Duncan.

Glimpses of this alter ego frequently snuck out. In junior high, I wore Roy Rogers pajamas to a church bake sale, telling customers our youth group was raising money to send me to a "special home." This was done, I might add, without the approval of my minister father.

I roller-skated through the halls of my high school wearing a clown suit and a mask of Richard Nixon. Again in college, I donned a mask and roller skates, only this time I wore a bikini and a signboard that read, "Follow me to Hoove's-A-Go-Go."

After college, I tried the corporate world, but quickly discovered that upper management tends to frown on flip-flops and high-top tennis shoes. I took to writing travel articles and personality profiles about people who make houses out of rolled-up newspapers, people who collect nuts and make films about guinea pigs.

As much as I like St. Francis of Assisi, I have come to the conclusion that I like wild people better. People who hug trees, ride Harleys, pierce their noses. People who live outside the bell curve. Either side of the bell curve.

Despite these glaring aberrations, I still feel like unflavored gelatin much of the time. Yes, I want to suck the marrow out of life, be Zorba the Greek. But at the same time, I want people to like me.

So I follow the rules. Mow my lawn. Watch my feet to make sure I'm doing it right.

I woke up one day to discover that my bold Isadora Duncan self had given way to a rote, lonely life. Instead of running with the wolves, I seemed to be crawling with the lemmings. My zany ideas, my outrageous dreams had been left to languish in the crisp green lawns of suburbia.

I don't really know how it happened. It's like the frog and the pot. You can't toss him in when the water's boiling. He'd jump out faster than you could say *french-fried frog legs*. But if you turn the heat up slowly, degree by tiny degree, he doesn't even notice he's being boiled alive.

Likewise, if "they"—whoever "they" are—tried to boil out our originality in one fell swoop, we'd put up our dukes immediately. But degree by tiny degree, we agree to conform, abandoning everything that's fun and original and authentically us.

This book is about breaking free, about jumping out of the boiling water no matter how long you've been cooked.

I've heard we teach what we want to know. In this case, I'm teaching what I want to do. I want to dress in angel costumes, travel without a suitcase, get up in the morning and decide who I am and what I want to be. I want to hang with other bohemians, people who value big ideas over big homes.

I want to meet friends in cafes to write. I want to spend Saturday nights painting on walls, hosting show-and-tells and playing charades. I want to share my dancing, daring, audacious side.

For years, I denied this side. I focused on this other person, this defective self. I was so busy doing affirmations, reading books, and trying to heal this broken-down impostor that I forgot the "real me," the crazy, quirky, lightning bug me, is the very thing I'd been searching for.

I hope *Art & Soul* is the very thing you've been searching for. It's about making art, yes. But it's also about becoming more, about recapturing that authentic self that many of us abandoned along with the Crayola crayons. Maybe yours isn't as bohemian or as "far out" as mine (creativity, after all, comes in many packages), but all of us have an authentic self that, over the years, has been broken into thousands of pieces just like our once-favorite blue-green crayon.

Most importantly, *Art & Soul* is the call to a spiritual path. Not only do we ask the bigger thing to shake and wake us up, but we trust that creating is our spiritual destiny, the road that leads us to enlightenment.

Author Bernie Siegel once went through a guided meditation to make contact with *his* inner guide. Since he's a Yale-educated medical doctor, you might suspect he'd radio in somebody famous, somebody like the Angel Gabriel or maybe a reincarnated Edie Sedgwick. Instead, he says, he got a guide named Frank.

Well, in this book, you get a guide named Pam, but I reckon between the two of us, the muses, and our prancing, creative spirits, we can do most anything.

CREATE. BOOGIE. SOAR..

OR, HOW THIS BOOK WORKS.

"Let's bare our arms and plunge deep, through laughter, through hope, into the very depths of our souls. Let's drag forth material crude, rough, neglected. Then let's sing it, dance it, write it, paint it. Let's do the impossible."

— AARON DOUGLAS, HARLEM RENAISSANCE PAINTER AND ILLUSTRATOR

This book is an apprenticeship, an actual yearlong journey into your creative soul.

Unlike some books that encourage you to uncover the negative gunk that stops you from creating, *Art & Soul* moves right to the heart: just do it! Not only will you find all kinds of offbeat, original activities like chalking poems on sidewalks and staging poetry readings around campfires, but each week you'll be invited to undertake a creative project such as a self-portrait or a song.

These projects are meant to be straightforward and painless.

That being said, I also recognize some of you might balk, might wonder why you're being asked to, say, doodle a giraffe.

But that's just cultural programming, the old story that says art shouldn't be taken seriously. The old story that insists composing a rap song is all rather pointless.

But I say, "Don't listen. Don't limit. Just do."

The projects run the gamut—from writing to the visual and performing arts, from singing to inventing a new business.

Give yourself permission to go crazy. Like Steve McQueen in *The Great Escape* when he jumps the barbed wire fence on his Triumph motorcycle, this book is a jailbreak. The projects offer a simple yet subversive arsenal of tools to change how you see yourself and how you interact with the world. They're meant to be fun, transformational, sometimes messy.

There isn't a lot of instruction. This is by design.

One of the main threads running through this book is "you don't need to know how." You've been to enough workshops. You've read enough books. Doing art is in your bones. It's in your makeup. You simply need to show up and listen. The universe will take care of the rest.

As filmmaker Jon Favreau likes to say, creativity is not something you control. It's something you access. It's with you all the time. This invisible, always-available creative spirit actively recruits humans like you to pilot in new and exciting projects. It continuously looks for physical beings to deliver inspiration to a starving-for-inspiration world.

And while it may not seem like it now, connecting with this "something bigger" is the most important thing you could ever do for yourself and indeed for all of mankind. I contend it's an inner need as important as food and shelter.

I have used this bigger thing to write 18 books, 2 screenplays, 4 plays, and a TV series. And I've done it by using a five-line invocation to the muses that I am about to share. Yours, of course, will be uniquely yours.

FACEBOOK WITH THE MUSES

"Possessing a creative mind, after all, is something like having a border collie for a pet: It needs to work, or else it will cause you an outrageous amount of trouble."

— ELIZABETH GILBERT, AUTHOR OF *BIG MAGIC*

Each of the 52 chapters (1 per week) features the aforementioned creative project, an inspirational message, and 3 additional . . . let's just call them zany activities.

But before you so much as pick up a paintbrush or a pencil or your tap-dancing toe, you're going to ask for help. You're going to assume that for every assignment, there's a team of guides who want to play along, spiritual teammates who have been waiting to come out and romp for a very long time.

So let's go over the two rudimentary but vital practices.

Practice One: Say Yes! The trick for luring the muses is pretty simple. *Show up.* That's it. That's the only requirement. Like anything with any value, creativity requires seat time. You'll compute your required daily time commitment in Week One.

The creative juice is equally available to everyone. It's like a water table underneath the earth that you tap into through discipline. All it takes to tap this unlimited pool is (a) desire

and (b) a willingness to show up and dig. It's truly that simple. Talent is beside the point.

Look at it from the muses' point of view. If you have an important project to present to the world, would you pick some two-timing, tap-dancing Willy too scared to commit? Or would you nominate the person who shows up every day, who is loyal, like the backyard dog?

Practice Two: Ask. This is where the invocation comes in. Once you have the muses' attention, simply ask them to use your skills, whatever they might be, in their service. Ask to be their channel. Agree to take dictation. Come at it humbly admitting you could use some assistance. In fact, your creative project for Week Two is to write your own personal invocation to the muses. Mine is a five-line plea I've been using for many years. I cut and paste it to the top of every project I undertake. I wouldn't dream of writing even a birthday card to my mother without its aid and assistance.

In addition to the projects, each week offers an essay on creativity and what I call Zumba for the Soul. These activities came straight off a big sheet of butcher block paper that I taped to the door in my basement office when my daughter Taz was four. Recognizing the weighty assignment of being a single parent, I was determined to do a good job raising her. But at the same time, I didn't want to lose my creative spark. I didn't want to surrender my free spirit. So on the door-long piece of paper, I magic-markered ideas I could undertake to keep my mojo going. Fun projects I could model, creative sparkplugs we could enjoy together.

Each week also includes a brief anecdote about a well-known artist, an artist who is successful, who has "made it." I call this part of the book "You're in Good Company," because you'll quickly come to realize that "real artists" are just like you—just as human, just as scared.

Many of us make the mistake of assuming the great masters get up each morning, pour a cup of coffee, and commence to pour out genius. Because they show us the stars and the moon and because they transport us to places we've never been, we forget that somebody had to pack a suitcase.

Remember when Dorothy's dog, Toto, pulls back the curtain hiding Oz, the great and terrible? After all that work getting the broom, all those encounters with flying monkeys, all that intimidation, Dorothy and her friends discover the Great Oz is an everyday Joe just like them.

Working artists haven't conquered their shaking knees. Sir Laurence Olivier suffered tremendous stage fright, John Steinbeck often felt like an impostor, and George Orwell endured a lifetime of unpopularity and insecurity.

In fact, the only real difference between you and "them" is they kept on scribbling and acting even when their hearts were pounding and their flying monkeys were squawking.

They kept at it. They asked. They said yes.

BATTLING YOUR INNER SALIERI

"Be Loki. Be Coyote. Be willing to stir the world's soup pot. Spit at the stars, show your backside to the council, whoop in church."

—JANE YODER, AUTHOR

If you saw the 1984 film *Amadeus*, you know all about Antonio Salieri, the Viennese court composer who had a, well . . . complicated relationship with Mozart. Recognizing the young composer's artistic gift, Salieri was intensely jealous of his young protégé and did everything he could to sabotage him.

That's why I call the voice that continually tries to defile every noble attempt at creating art my Inner Salieri. It's the voice that puts a roadblock between me and everything the higher forces ask me to do. The voice that tells me I'm not good enough to produce anything of value. The wily foe that, in my opinion, is the root cause of all the world's depression and unhappiness.

The good news is that, with discipline, you can sweep it into a cage and become its warden. The essays for the following 13 weeks outline the many guises this enemy will take. It's important to know them going in. Arming yourself against your Inner Salieri is a day-by-day process, one that can only succeed by showing up, staring it down, asking for help, and opening the trench coat to the real you, the naked you inside.

WEEK 1

SHINE

"This little light of mine. I'm going to let it shine."

— CHRISTIAN SPIRITUAL

Most books tell you how to get something—a sizzling sex life, thinner thighs, a higher return on your investment dollars. *Art & Soul* is a book that tells you how to give, how to reach deep inside yourself and pull out the artistic blessing that is yours to give. The blessing no one else can give.

Maybe it's a poem tapping on your heart. Maybe there's a song that keeps you awake at night, a business idea that won't leave you alone. A dream you keep pushing aside with some thought like, *Nah! I could never sing or dance like that. I could never start a business.*

Now is the time to quit pushing that dream aside.

Every dream that has ever tiptoed across your mind is a summons from the universe. A summons that says, "I need you."

On the day you were born, you were presented with a creative gift. It is a gift the world needs. Your song may never be sung on *Jimmy Fallon*. It may never make the Top 40. But somebody out there needs to hear it. Maybe it's the 92-year-old shut-in who lives next door, who giggles every time she overhears you sing, "I wish I were an Oscar Mayer weiner" outside her bedroom window. Isn't that enough?

At times, it seems like a daunting task, adding your voice to the chorus. You wonder:

What do I have to add to the world's great body of art?

Who am I to join the likes of Michelangelo, James Cameron, Prince?

I would suggest the better question is this: Who are you not to? What right do you have to refuse the voice that whispers to you every morning, every afternoon, and every evening as you retire spent and exhausted from denying again and again the hand of the Great Collaborator?

But hasn't everything already been said?

Until we hear your version of this fierce and joyful world, there is more to be said. Each man looks upon the sunset with a slightly different eye.

All of us long for a rich, participatory life. We all have the same recurrent longing to break down our defenses, to be able to give and receive our gifts. When we compose a piece of music or shape a lump of clay, we wriggle out of the straitjacket and come out shouting "yes, yes, yes" to life's unlimited, unceasing possibilities.

Alexander Papaderos, who started a monastery and peace center in Crete, Greece, carries a piece of a broken mirror in his wallet. When he was a small boy, he found the mirror next to a motorcycle that someone had wrecked and abandoned near his small village. He spent hours trying to put it back together. Unfortunately, some of the pieces were missing so he had little choice but to give up, but not before plucking out the biggest piece, which he rubbed against a rock until it was smooth and round. Papaderos spent much of his childhood playing with that piece of mirror. He discovered that when he held it just right, he could shine the sun's light into the dark, lighting up unknown cracks and crevices.

That's what this book is all about. Your piece of the mirror is just a fragment. Nobody knows for sure how big and vast "the whole" really is. But if you take your small piece and hold it just right, you can shine light into the world's dark places.

The choice is yours. You can use your mirror to shine light. Or you can keep it in your wallet. But the mirror will never be whole without you.

Just Do It

ANALYZE YOUR TIME

*"Do you have the courage to grab
the dreams that picked you?"*

— PRINCE EA, POET AND RAPPER

Since this is the year where your life is going to explode open
(in the best possible way), let's start with a little creative in-
vestigation.

For the next week, simply log the amount of time you
spend on Facebook, Twitter, and other social media. That's it.
Just write down the number of minutes (hours?) you spend
liking, commenting, and scrolling through status updates.

According to 2015 analytics (and I'm sure it has only gone
up), the average Facebook user spends 40 minutes trawling
per day. You might also want to note your time expenditure
staring at a box. That is, your television set.

Next week, after you've got a handle on the amount of
time you spend on these two activities, you're going to surrender half of that time (say 20 minutes, if you're in the national average) to commune with what artists over the years
have called the muses. I guarantee the stuff you'll discover

SHINE

is far more interesting, entertaining, and life-changing than anything you'll ever find on Facebook.

In addition to keeping track of your time, get a cheap notebook and jot down three ideas every day. They can be about anything. They don't have to be good. They might even be terrible. And that's perfectly okay. The practice is simply a workout for your imagination.

In my journal, along with my to-do lists and daily musings, I note three new ideas. Every single day. Sometimes they're ridiculous. Like a purse that's black on one side and brown on the other so you can match your shoes depending on which side faces outward. Sometimes, they're far beyond my desire to implement, like my idea to start a national clothing exchange between people of the same size, so you get a wide-ranging wardrobe without contributing to the 10.5 million tons of clothes that end up in landfills each year. Other times, my ideas are meaningful and I actually do them. Like giving something away every day. Every now and again, they're pure genius. Like a new book or screenplay idea, one of which you're holding in your hand.

The point isn't to judge. It's to exercise your atrophied imagination. Just like your body needs physical therapy to walk after lying flat on your back for two weeks, your idea muscle, which has dried up from lack of use, needs imagination therapy.

Trust me on this. It will change every aspect of your life. You'll be sharper, quicker, more prolific. You'll be happier, more curious. When you need a good idea (say you lose an important client or you're planning a birthday party), it'll be a cakewalk to call one up. When your idea muscle is a lean, mean fighting machine, it provides countless new trailheads to explore, multitudinous new portals through your mental architecture.

Zumba for the Soul

- Go to a thrift store and buy the most outrageous outfit you can.
- Learn three little-known facts about Martin Luther King Jr.
- Make sugar cookies shaped like body parts.

You're in Good Company

Even with all his success, Steven Spielberg still suffers from insecurity. He says it's like having big ears—it doesn't change because you win an Oscar.

WEEK 2

KNOW THY ENEMY

"For the first couple years you make stuff, it's just not that good. It's trying to be good, it has potential to be good, but it's not. A lot of people never get past this phase. They quit. Most people who do interesting, creative work went through years of this."

— IRA GLASS, PRODUCER OF *THIS AMERICAN LIFE*

As much as you want to sit down, grab your paintbrush, and start producing beautiful pieces of art, let me just say that it's probably not going to happen. At first.

When you first commit to this course of daily spirituality, a lot of embarrassing and uncomfortable things are going to happen. It's nothing to be alarmed about. It's just that right now, you're rusty. You're out of shape.

You have no idea what to paint or write or draw. You probably don't hear a damn thing from your muses. You just have this faint inkling that you want to create something, this tiny whisper that insists you have something to say.

Let me assure you that you do. You have something important to say, something the world needs to hear.

That conviction is sometimes enough to keep people going.

Usually it's not.

The cold truth is there are a lot of alligators in the pond.

This week, we're going to look those enemies straight in the whites of their eyes. We're going to examine what we're up against. What every artist is up against. Even Maya Angelou, the prolific author who wrote dozens of books, claimed that every single time she started a new one, she experienced the same fear, the same questioning. Can she do it again? It's always a scary proposition.

So picture me as the football coach—with a diagram of the opponents in this week's game. Yeah, they're big. Yeah, they're tough. But remember, the Creative Spirit is always stronger.

Enemy #1—Procrastination. When you first commit to working on your art, you will hear a tiny voice. Or at least you'll think you did. Or you did until the appointed hour arrives. And then it's, *What was I thinking? I want to be an artist, but not today. Probably tomorrow.* And then you go on living the same life you've been living before, the same life from which you want to escape.

When you first begin to hear the artists' call, every single excuse will come up. You'd rather do most anything than work on your art. Collecting discarded toenail clippings will sound like the very highest form of entertainment. You'd rather scrub the kitchen floor or cut the balls off your vintage wool sweater than sit down at the computer like you promised yourself.

That's your rut—the life that's not working, the life you want to change.

Enemy #2—Resistance. Change is uncomfortable. Especially something this risky. Every artist is on the tightwire. No longer cowering. No longer hiding.

Every cell in your body is going to resist. You've suddenly made a 360-degree turn and the muscles in your psyche, the wires in your neural chemistry, are going to put up their dukes. You can count on it.

Expect the conflict, the interruptions, the excuses, the self-doubt.

Anne Lamott says when she sits down to write, she immediately begins to wonder if she needs orthodontia. Once she called her brother to see if he had noticed a new mole on her neck.

Quite wisely, he said, "Annie, get back to work."

Because that's the only thing that will get you through it. There's no other way. You can't will your art to appear. You've got to be there and you've got do it every day.

Would you hire an employee that sometimes showed up for work, sometimes didn't? The muses have lots of stories and songs and paintings to give the world, but they can only work through someone who shows up.

Enemy #3—Self-doubt. You'll hate everything you produce. You'll look at whatever it is and think, "This is pure drivel. I'd be wise to stop."

While proving yourself, you're going to get a lot of junk that will embarrass you, that makes you think, *I have no talent.*

The good news is it will get better. It will get easier.

It takes practice. It takes a lot of time being crippled and scared and not sure why you ever wanted to get involved in this crazy "creativity business" in the first place.

So just say *hallelujah.* The more junk you write or draw or paint, the sooner you'll tap into the good stuff. It's not always pretty. It's not always fun. But there's an angel in that piece of marble. And it's up to you to keep chipping and chiseling and pounding.

Just do it!

WRITE AN INVOCATION TO THE MUSES.

"Don't worry about mistakes. There aren't any."
— MILES DAVIS, MUSICIAN

I created my invocation to the muses after reading Steven Pressfield's excellent book *The War of Art*. I've given away many, many copies and I reread it at least once a year. Pressfield says his most important ritual is a daily prayer to the Muse, uttered out loud in absolute earnest. Using the start of Homer's *Odyssey*, he appeals to "O Divine Poesy, Goddess daughter of Zeus."

Here's mine:

Oh, great muses, I open myself now to be your channel. I put aside all preconceived notions about myself, about the world and about what I am meant to write. I surrender to your wisdom. Thank you for giving me this opportunity to receive and pass on your gifts. I set them free to go out and bless the universe. Amen.

Zumba for the Soul

- Invent a new type of soup.
- Name a rock band.
- Paint your fingernails 10 different colors.

You're in Good Company

Oprah was fired from her job as cub reporter for Baltimore's WJZ-TV. She was told she was too emotional and unfit for TV.

NIKE WAS RIGHT

"But there it sits, nevertheless, calmly licking its chops."
— H. L. MENCKEN, JOURNALIST, SATIRIST,
AND CULTURAL CRITIC

Once you get a feel for this book, you'll probably conclude the important part is the inspirational messages. You'll read them with religious fervor, feel inspired, be ready to take on the world. You'll feel sure you're destined to become a great artist, to produce masterpieces that drive others to their knees.

The weekly projects, hey, they sound fun, too, but I'll do them later . . . when I have a free moment. Probably tomorrow.

Let me clear something up for you. The weekly essays are not the important part of this book.

In *Dead Poets Society*, Mr. Keating, the English teacher played by Robin Williams, asks his students to turn to a section on analyzing poetry. As one of the boys begins read-ing, Keating jumps wildly out of his chair.

"Rip that introduction out," he yells to the incredulous students. "It's horsesh*t. Be gone with it."

That's how I feel about these messages. I like them. In fact, they were my weekly projects for a year. But you'll miss the whole point of this book if you pass on the projects. It'd be like going to the rodeo and ignoring the horses.

Yet, I know a lot of you won't do the creative project. Oh, you'll want to. You'll mean to. You'll keep adding it to your to-do list. But then it gets late. And you're tired. And your very favorite comedian is going to be on *Colbert* . . . and, well, you'll just do it tomorrow.

If I had done all the things I dreamed about doing, I'd have a Pulitzer, an Oscar, and a note from God informing the world that I was the most functional (as opposed to dysfunc-tional) person on this planet.

What I'm trying to say is I've got your number. So let me just reiterate: the creative projects are what make this book special. They're the gift, the meat and potatoes, the real rea-son you're here with me today.

One of the most personally influential books in my library is *The Artist's Way* by Julia Cameron. Twice, I've been in Art-ist's Way groups. This is a suggestion she made that I actually *did* follow. She recommends we artists band together and support one another.

The first time I took the class (a 12-week course follow-ing each of the chapters), I loved it. I'd have rather poked a rusty fork in my eye than miss the Saturday morning session. I lived for the next week so I could talk about my angst over "not writing" or how I was shamed by my grade-school art teacher. It was group therapy, but I don't remember that my output increased. I didn't grow as an artist or become a better writer.

The second time, however, was a different story. First of all, I was facilitating the group. So I had this pressure to actually *be* an artist. Out of frustration on the first day of class (there were so many attendees I couldn't keep track), I asked everyone to make a name tag.

No big deal, right?

Well, ask an artist to make anything and watch out. The results were astounding. Each member bought in a beautiful name tag that expressed their uniqueness. In that second class, we spent less time talking about our childhood issues and more time talking about the wild variety of media we used with our name tags.

From that point on, we did a project every week. We still spent the first hour of our two-hour session talking about our blocks and struggles, but the last hour was spent performing a character or reading a poem or showing a self-portrait.

It was powerful. People started changing. They started doing their art. It was particularly freeing to work in other media. As a writer, I feel responsible for sticking with projects that make me look good. But I could paint and not give a rat's ass what anybody thought.

Once we committed to being there for our art, our muses showed up in full regalia. I could almost hear them talking among themselves. "You know, I think we can count on these people."

Brilliant things began to pour forth.

One night, at 3 A.M., a children's book, something I'd never aspired to write, yanked me by the arm. Daniel began painting bright, kicky portraits and got dozens of new commissions. Bonnie started writing poetry that helped her

through a nasty divorce. Beth started drawing after a several-year hiatus.

So that's why it's important to do the creative projects.

It's fine to dream about painting or writing a stage play, but unless you actually sit down and work at it, nothing will ever change.

~~~~~~~~~~~~~~~~~~~~

Just do it!

MAKE AN ARTIST'S AMULET

"The big question is whether you are going to be able to say a hearty yes to your adventure."

— JOSEPH CAMPBELL, AMERICAN MYTHOLOGIST WHO COINED THE TERM "FOLLOW YOUR BLISS"

You'll probably recognize your fellow artists by the gleam in their eye. They look bouncier somehow, more joyful, more playful. They don't quite fit the mold society tries to squish us into.

But just so the rest of the world will know, make yourself an amulet—some special pin or badge or tie—that identifies yourself as an *Art & Soul* participant. Proclaim to the world that you are an artist.

Zumba for the Soul

- Create a new bar drink.
- Paint a pair of old tennis shoes.
- Eat breakfast somewhere you've never eaten before.

You're in Good Company

Every cartoon Charles Schulz, the creator of the wildly popular *Peanuts* comic strip, submitted to his high school yearbook was unanimously rejected.

WEEK 4

YOU ALREADY KNOW HOW

"If a man wants to be sure of his road he must close his eyes and walk in the dark."

— St. John of the Cross, mystic and saint

The first thing most of us do when pursuing a new art is find a class, buy a book, seek out the advice of an expert. While there's certainly a time and place for outside help, that's usually not the most prudent path on which to begin.

When we go outside seeking direction, we create at least two hurdles. The obvious one is the time we waste. Instead of leaping in when the idea is fresh, when its voice demands to be heard, we put it off, insist it be patient and wait until we learn how to punctuate sentences or mix paint. We ask this burning, passionate idea that wants nothing but to dance and scream to sit quietly outside the door and wait.

But it can't wait.

Think of the idea that's knocking on your door as a small child. It can't understand that grown-ups have other things to do.

"But," you insist, "I really don't know how. I have never written an article, let alone a book. I have never created a character, let alone a whole play. I need help."

This may sound like a rational plea. But I assure you, it's a stall tactic. Sure, your reason for waiting may seem reasonable and mature, but you're dealing with an idea that is anything but reasonable and mature. In fact, if you do wait, it will become reasonable and mature. But who wants to see a reasonable and mature sculpture? A reasonable and mature stage play?

The juice, the gas has turned into an adult.

You can polish your skills later—after the idea that's pounding in your skull has been aired. Get it down now.

Waiting until you know how can take a week if you read a book, a semester if you take a class, a lifetime if you perfect a skill. By then, the idea is stiff and lifeless. It's as faded as the old gingham curtains hanging in the kitchen window.

Once the fire is gone, we have a great excuse not to write at all, or if we do persist, we get discouraged by the stiffness and wonder where we missed the boat. Guess we should take another class.

It's imperative to answer the questions when they're first asked. Otherwise, they have no choice but to look elsewhere. They must find someone who has the time and the confidence to carry the torch.

Sam Shepard, who has written more than 40 plays, was 21 when he wrote his first 2 plays, *Cowboys* and *The Rock Garden*. As a young artist living in New York, he had no formal theater training and no exposure to dramatic literature.

Luckily for him, he was too naïve and inexperienced to question whether he knew how to write a play—nobody had told him yet that people don't write a new play every two weeks. Instead, he listened to the fierce male characters hopscotching through his head. If he'd have said, "Hey, guys, I hear you, but I'm kinda busy right now with this class. I'll go to the library tomorrow and see if I can find a book," the American theater scene would be missing 40 controversial and poignant plays.

Don't head off to the bookstore. Don't call the college to see when the next gouache class is. Jump in. Get your feet wet. Place your faith in the idea itself. It has the ability to teach you anything you need to know. Within its fiery beat are both the questions *and* the answers. If you surrender to the idea, it will take you home.

Start now.

Just do it!

TRANSFORM A FLAT PIECE OF
PAPER INTO A 3-D OBJECT

*"Society gave me a ten-foot wall and a five-foot ladder
and then sat back to see if I'd get my black ass over that
wall. It wasn't impossible, but I had to be creative."*

— TRACY MORGAN, COMEDIAN

This is the place to write down your favorite excuse.

The one you use to justify why you haven't yet plunged
in. We are, after all, on Week 4.

_____

_____

_____

_____

_____

Popular choices:

1. Not enough time.

2. Not enough money.

3. Not enough support from family/lover/friends.

Which is why I'm about to tell you the story of Tracy Morgan, the Emmy-nominated actor and *Saturday Night Live* superstar. His story will put whatever crazy excuse you just wrote down in perspective.

Not only did Tracy grow up in an impoverished inner city housing project, but his dad was a heroin addict, his mom dragged him to casinos on school nights, and he got married when he was 19. Oh, and did I mention he sold crack cocaine?

"If you think about it, I really shouldn't be here at all. If you're the kind of person who likes numbers and statistics, I'm the long shot," he says.

Indeed, many of his friends didn't make it. They tripped out, got popped in the head, or were blasted by the wrong end of a hot-headed drug dealer's .357. By 16, he needed both hands to count all the casualties.

Being funny, he says, wasn't a career choice. It was a way to survive.

After his dad died of AIDS, he dropped out of high school and began hustling—weed, concessions at Yankee Stadium, burgers at Wendy's—anything he could come up with to support his wife and, now, three kids.

Through it all, he relied on his "big mouth and funny face." In other words, his gift, the thing he could do better than nearly anyone else.

After crowds started gathering outside his favorite chicken shop to listen to him "make fun of sh*t," he came up with a dream that changed his life.

"I started thinking to myself, how much different could it be, standing up there onstage?"

When he told Sabina, his then wife, about his unlikely career choice, he expected her to react the way his family and friends did—laughing like it was the best joke of all.

Instead she said, "I think you should do it."

And then she looked deeply into his eyes and added, "But if you're going to do it, Tray, you've got to be focused. You've got to do it all the way."

"I will always love her for that," Morgan says. "She could have easily turned over one night and said, 'Motherf*cker, UPS is hiring.' That would have been the last the world heard of Tracy Morgan."

So now . . . you be Tracy and I'll be Sabina.

And that excuse? Rip it right out of this book (tear a page out of a magazine if you're reading this digitally) and turn it into origami.

Zumba for the Soul

- ✻ Catch a jar of fireflies. (If it's winter, make a chorus of snow angels.)

- ✻ Wear nothing but yellow or purple or blue.

- ✻ See how many Christmas carols you can remember.

You're in Good Company

Donald Sutherland has made more than 100 films, but he still gets so nervous, he throws up before filming begins.

DARE TO BE MEDIOCRE

"It ain't easy being green."

— KERMIT THE FROG, A MUPPET

"The more failures, the more successes. Period."

— TOM PETERS, AUTHOR OF
IN SEARCH OF EXCELLENCE

Okay, now for the good news. You have permission to write, draw, and paint the worst crap in America. Not only do you have blanket amnesty, you have the responsibility to write lots of garbage, paint lots of blobs, and dance like a tin soldier.

When we allow ourselves to be beginners, to be mediocre, we plunge into new territory. The muse requires nothing less.

To be a beginner, an artist who isn't perfect, takes bravery. To make a mess takes balls. Only those willing to plug their noses, to dive in naked, earn the privilege of courting the muse.

What muse in her right mind would hook up with some anal retentive perfectionist who has to be Georgia O'Keeffe or William Shakespeare first time out. People like that won't take risks. They're cramped and stiff. The muse seeks people who will step off the cliff, people who aren't afraid to look stupid.

Those who want to do it perfectly have an agenda. And the truth is we don't have enough information to judge. We don't really know what's good or bad, let alone what's perfect.

When I wrote my fourth book, a self-published weight-loss book eventually bought by Simon & Schuster, I needed a drawing to demonstrate the importance of deep breathing. I drew this primitive woman who bore a striking resemblance to George Washington. To my powers of judgment, it was absolutely the world's worst drawing. If I wasn't on a shoestring budget, if I'd had even 25 more dollars, I'd have begged some graphic design student to redo it.

Able to console myself with the fact that I was a writer, not an artist, I said screw it and let it be.

The drawing, which to this day is infantile and unprofessional, received lots of comments. Dozens of people came up to me later and told me how much they liked it. The only thing I can figure is it demonstrated my vulnerability. It opened the curtain to a piece of me.

The point is I wasn't capable of judging which art was good or bad. Or rather, I wasn't able to judge what bad art (yes, it was bad) might move someone, might need to be said.

Be willing to be vulnerable. Give up any investment in what the neighbors think.

Even the most renowned artists make messes. As Anne Lamott once said, "We all feel like we're pulling teeth. Even for the best of writers, the right words and sentences do not come flowing out like ticker tape."

The trick she says is to get something . . . anything . . . down.

She calls it writing "sh*tty first drafts." If you write lots of terrible first drafts, "You'd learn that good second drafts can spring from these, and you'd see that big sloppy imperfect messes have value."

Messes, like compost piles, are fertile, brimming and beating with life.

One year, an unidentified nonflying vine sprouted from my compost pile. For months, I watched it wind around the garden, eagerly awaiting its first blossom, wondering what vegetable I'd inadvertently planted. Finally, it appeared, green and spotty. I assumed it was a zucchini.

One morning, I plucked it from the vine to make zucchini bread. My neighbor who was outside hosing down her two-year-old said, "Wow! What a funny-looking pumpkin."

So, no, I didn't get zucchini bread. But, I got one of the best jack-o'-lantern pumpkins in the neighborhood.

The point is, we don't know. We just have to show up.

Just do it!

COME UP WITH THE TITLE (JUST THE TITLE) OF YOUR FORTHCOMING MEMOIR

"As my artist's statement explains, my work is utterly incomprehensible and is therefore full of deep significance"

— CALVIN (FROM *CALVIN AND HOBBES*, AS CHANNELED BY BILL WATTERSON)

Mindy Kaling called hers *Is Everyone Hanging Out Without Me?* Cheryl Strayed called her poignant tale of walking the Pacific Crest Trail *Wild*. Katharine Hepburn was famous enough to get away with calling hers simply *Me*. What are you going to call your memoir?

Zumba for the Soul

- Make a hat out of newspaper.
- Write 500 words about someone you hate.
- Plan your vacation to your favorite Caribbean island. Make rum punches and get straw hats to celebrate.

You're in Good Company

J.K. Rowling was divorced, bankrupt, and on welfare when Bloomsbury finally agreed to publish *Harry Potter and the Philosopher's Stone*. Her editor, after 11 other publishers rejected it, suggested she get a "real job" because "there's no money in children's books."

41

WEEK 6

FEAR AND INSECURITY, BE GONE! I'VE GOT BRILLIANCE TO CREATE.

"The assumption that art is a regal robe which falls upon your shoulders magically, bestowed upon you as an heir apparent rather than achieved through slinging the pickax across your shoulder every morning and making off to the mine, was revealed as the greatest hindrance of all to artistic work."

—JANE LAZARRE, AUTHOR OF *THE MOTHER KNOT*

This is a story about discipline. And about quaking in my boots.

In the run-up to the release of *E-Squared*, Hay House FedExed a book called *Platform*. They insisted it was required reading. Social media, a marketing bonanza of which even the smallest of authors can take advantage, can be leveraged through daily blogging, says its author, Michael Hyatt.

I'd heard this before. Popular author and marketer Seth Godin claims blogging is one of the most important practices of his profession. He says it clarifies his thoughts, forces him to notice things, and gives him a forum for talking to his fans.

To commit to writing a blog a day was thrilling and terrifying at the same time.

Thrilling because, my gosh, I've wanted to be disciplined enough to write daily for as long as I've been able to hold a pencil. It's the linchpin that holds a writer together—consistency, daily attendance to the muses, and well, the simple act of applying the old rear end to the chair. I'd used it countless times when writing the 18 books that have my name on them.

However, when I'm not on assignment or expected by some editor to deliver the goods, I don't always write. Even though I know the only way to truly call yourself a writer is to write. Even though I know the importance of showing up for the muses, day after day.

I faithfully showed up, all right, but only when editors gave me deadlines, only when my bank balance needed heft.

That's why I was terrified. Blogging every day felt like streaking in front of a crowded arena. Granted, my subscriber list at the time amounted to my mom and a couple friends, but I knew if I did it right, I might create a following. That's a scary proposition.

Hunters call it buck fever—that unexplained paralysis that sets in when they're face-to-face with the big one.

Why would anyone want to follow me? Who am I to command respect? Yes, I suffer massive insecurity even though I'm what the world might call a successful writer. I've sold and written 18 books. I've been on big TV talk shows. I write for the kind of national magazines you find in dentists' offices. Yet, I'm still terrified.

But when was terror ever a decent reason to cut off your brilliance? All terror really means is you're listening to the wrong voice.

Both voices, always there. Your Inner Salieri? Or the voice of your true calling, your magnificence?

Just do it!

START A BLOG

*"Show up, show up, show up and
after a while, the muse shows up, too."*

— ISABEL ALLENDE, AUTHOR

Writing a blog is free, priceless, and, according to Seth Godin, one the best things you could ever do for yourself. He recommends writing a blog post a day, the perfect project for this week.

Don't panic, a blog can be a paragraph or two.

A couple guidelines:

1. Write like you talk. You don't fret about how to talk, do you?

2. Simply notice things. Writing a blog for seven days straight will jar you into paying attention to life's humor and limitless beauty.

3. Blog for the love of it. Resist all urges to monetize.

4. Establish what motivates you to get out of bed. What are you passionate about?

Zumba for the Soul

※ Make yourself a pair of angel wings.

※ Find and read three poems by Rumi.

※ Eat lunch somewhere unusual—maybe in a tree?

You're in Good Company

Lady Gaga, whose hits have topped charts in nearly every category, got dropped by Def Jam Recordings a short three months after they signed her.

BABY STEPS

"Don't stop biting your fingernails. Just stop biting one."

— SONNY KRASNER, COMEDIAN

And now for my first number . . .

When we sit down to tackle our first project, most of us have something in mind like winning a Grammy or painting the next *Mona Lisa*. But this is like trying to swim the Atlantic.

You're bound to run into tidal waves and icebergs, your muscles are going to cramp, and you're probably going to give up before you get to Bermuda. A better strategy is to begin with the swimming pool in the backyard.

This week, we're going to talk about something you mastered in kindergarten. Remember Mother, May I? Remember baby steps?

Those tiny, two-inch shuffles got you to the finish line just as effectively as bunny hops, scissors steps, or what you thought you wanted—giant steps.

When writing her first book, Jan Steward was feeling overwhelmed until a friend dropped by with a piece of bead-work from India. It was 10 inches wide and 30 feet long, and it illustrated a complicated love story complete with court-ship, wedding, and final escape from both lovers' families. It was made from beads the size of sesame seeds.

Steward took one look at it and asked, "How on earth could a person ever do this?"

Her friend rubbed his chin thoughtfully and answered, "Well, I think first you take a white bead . . ."

All you have to do for today is take that first white bead. Make one little baby step in the direction of your dream. It doesn't have to be huge—maybe it's writing a description of your character's hot pink negligee or drawing a quick sketch of just one daffodil. Don't even think about what the charac-ter might say to her mother when she walks in with a bag of groceries or about that pregnant bumblebee buzzing around the daffodil's pistil.

For now, writing about the character's negligee is enough. Give that negligee everything you've got. The rest, for the time being, doesn't matter.

Just one step. Just one bead.

If you do it any other way, you're gonna drown. You're going to hit that first iceberg, throw up your hands, and say, "I quit." Writing a novel or sculpting an angel is overwhelming.

But by taking it bead by bead, day after day, you can get clear across the Atlantic. Put a few beads on every day—put them on like you might practice scales on a piano. Do it as a debt of honor.

It's this daily beadwork that builds muscle. Just like the weight lifter who bulks up his triceps and biceps by pumping iron day after day, you develop creative muscle—the stamina, the sense of honor that will get you across the Atlantic—by daily practice.

It's important to see these tiny steps as tools, to think of yourself as a carpenter or a cement layer. Trying to be an artist is enough to freeze anyone. Trying to make something that will be admired for centuries is enough to stop a bull charging for a red cape.

Once when interviewing Sir Laurence Olivier, Barbara Walters asked him how he wanted to be remembered.

"As a workman," he replied.

She was surprised. "Don't you want us to think of you as an actor or an artist?"

"No," he went on, "That doesn't matter. Shakespeare was a workman, poets are workmen. God is a workman and that is how I wish to be remembered."

So put on your overalls, tie up your boots, and mount that first rung of the ladder. Step by step. It'll take you all the way to the stars.

Just do it!

WRITE A SIX-WORD MEMOIR.
NO MORE. NO LESS.

*"Creation is a better means of self-expression
than possession. It is through creating,
not possessing that life is revealed."*

— VIDA D. SCUDDER, ENGLISH POET

Once asked to write a full story in six words, Ernest Hemingway responded: "For Sale: baby shoes, never worn."

So this week, we're shooting for simple and profound brevity. Not that there's any pressure.

Here are a few examples from the book *Not Quite What I Was Planning*, a collection of six-word memoirs.

Author Dave Eggers: *Fifteen years since last professional haircut.*

Singer Aimee Mann: *Couldn't cope so I wrote songs.*

Comedian Stephen Colbert: *Well, I thought it was funny.*

Zumba for the Soul

❁ Spend two hours in a hammock doing nothing.

❁ Record yourself acting out a scene from *It's a Wonderful Life*.

❁ Find the best vantage point possible and watch the sunset.

You're in Good Company

Isabel Allende had to publish three novels before she felt comfortable putting "writer" rather than "housewife" in the space for "occupation" when filling out a form. *Writer* was such a big word, she explained.

WEEK 8

SUMMONING THE MUSES

"Shiver awake now at the doing of your dream . . ."

— BOB SAVINO, POET AND KANSAS CITY SAGE

The trick for luring the muses is simple.

It has two words.

Show up.

It you want to write or paint or make a film, you've got to set a time and be there.

The muses will let you set your own hours, but you've got to set the hours. You've got to convince them you're serious. Dreaming about writing a book will not get the book written. Reading books about painting will not get the painting painted.

The muses are eager to deliver the goods, but you've got to prove you're serious. You've got to show up.

When you think about it, it's exciting news. It takes the onus off having to possess some extraordinary talent. Isn't that what we're afraid of? That we're not as literarily adept as Toni Morrison, as skillful as Meryl Streep?

When I read anything by Pat Conroy, I feel about two inches tall. I want to hide, take any reference to "writer" off my resume. I recently read Mary Karr's memoir *Lit*. It was so beautifully written, I was tempted to throw in the towel. Compared to her, I'm a neophyte, a plebeian nobody.

Well, that isn't the point. The reason those writers perform with such eloquence is because they've put in the time. They've practiced over and over again.

They've been there through thick and thin. They've written every day when there were other things they could have been doing. They've written when it wasn't convenient, when they felt they didn't measure up, when they thought they were as talented as a jar of pickled onions. They convinced their muses they were loyal devotees.

In music, the connection between genius and time spent is obvious. Let's say the muses, looking to deliver a stunning new piece of music, have two candidates—the guy who bought a guitar three months ago but still hasn't picked it up or the guy who has been practicing for 10 years. The muses have little choice but to go with loyalty. They must bestow their masterpiece to the guy with the technical ability to play it.

Madeleine L'Engle once wrote about a small village in Bavaria. When the village clockmaker died, leaving no children or apprentices, all the clocks and the watches of the village eventually, over time, broke down. Years later, a renowned clockmaker showed up and everyone rushed to him begging him to fix their broken-down timepieces. The wise old clockmaker, who only had so much time, looked at the abandoned timepieces and finally announced he would only fix the ones that had been kept wound. They were the only ones, he said, that would remember how to keep time.

We may not be able to make our clocks run perfectly, but at least we can get up every day and wind them so they won't forget.

Just do it!

INVENT A CREATIVITY RITUAL

*"The paths we can't yet visualize are
the ones we should get excited about."*

— KELLY BROGAN, AMERICAN PHYSICIAN

Like many great scientific advances, Pavlovian conditioning was discovered accidentally.

Russian physiologist Ivan Pavlov noticed his dogs salivated every time he entered the room, even when he wasn't carrying their dog bowls.

Create some ritual to perform before you begin your projects. Maybe play a particular song. Or light a candle. It doesn't matter what it is.

It's simply a sleight of hand that tricks your imagination into salivating.

John Cheever used to put on his business suit, leave his apartment, and go to his basement where he hung his suit on a hanger and wrote in his underwear. Friedrich Schiller couldn't write unless his bare feet were immersed in cold water. Jack Kerouac wrote by candlelight. David Lynch goes to the same Bob's Big Boy every day at 2:30 and drinks a giant chocolate milkshake for the rush of ideas.

Zumba for the Soul

- ❋ Make a sock monkey or some other stuffed animal.

- ❋ Buy a gift for less than $5 and wrap it creatively. Don't forget to give it away.

- ❋ Draw a picture of your first-grade classroom.

You're in Good Company

Actor Ryan Reynolds, once chosen as *People* magazine's Sexiest Man Alive, said, "I feel like an overweight, pimply faced kid a lot of the time."

WEEK 9

FINDING TIME

"What are best things and worst things in your life and when are you going to get around to whispering them or shouting them?"

— RAY BRADBURY, SCIENCE FICTION AND FANTASY AUTHOR

Say it one last time if you must, but after this week, you will never again utter the world's most famous excuse:

"I don't have time."

I'm not denying that most of us are overcommitted, over-stretched, overburdened.

But I do have to ask this question: "Why?"

Do you really need your nails done every week? Do you really need to gossip with your sister every night? Are those reruns of *Seinfield* really that important to your well-being?

This week, we're going to develop a strategy for scraping out time to write your novel, practice your guitar, take those long-lusted-after acting lessons.

Don't expect some unoriginal suggestion such as "get up 30 minutes earlier" or "devote the last 15 minutes of your lunch hour to developing plot points." You can figure out those ho-hum strategies on your own. Heck, you probably tried the "get up 30 minutes early strategy" last New Year's when you resolved to yoga to Rodney Yee every morning.

No, my tip is stay in bed 30 minutes longer. Spend that time dreaming. Fill yourself with magic. When mystery and passion fill your soul, finding time is as easy as signing up for Twitter.

Gandhi used to say that if he had a busy day, he had little choice but to add meditation to his to-do list. Otherwise, he'd never get everything done.

Strategy #2: Make the novel, the screenplay—whatever it is you want to work on—*no big deal*. The real reason most of us can't find time is our annoying tendency toward perfectionism. If the novel doesn't have to read like James Joyce, we could probably sneak in a sentence or two between appointments, while the kids are playing hide-and-seek in the basement.

So instead of waiting for time, steal it like an ornery eight-year-old who shoves a cookie in his pocket the minute Mom looks the other way. Steal it while you're waiting for the train, on your coffee break, while your husband is plucking his nose hairs.

The old "I'll do it when I have time . . ." is a fairy tale, like Santa Claus and the tooth fairy. Wake up, Virginia. Huge lump sums of time do not exist.

Lawyer Scott Turow was able to write all 431 pages of his bestseller *Presumed Innocent* on the Chicago commuter train. Stephenie Meyer, whose Twilight series has sold over 100 million copies, plotted her novels during her kids' swimming lessons.

Strategy three: Give up self-sabotage. I find that if I give up self-loathing (a sport in which I've won several gold medals), I have all kinds of free time. It takes gallons of energy to continually tell myself what an excrementitious piece of monkey vomit I am. Each of us gets only so many units of energy. If we use up 35 or more of our allotted 100 units on low-flying shame, guilt, and the realization that yesterday's 4 pages need to be carved into thousands of tiny pieces, we only have 65 valuable energy units left.

And while we're on the subject, let's move to number four, which is give up every single thing that isn't enriching your life. C'mon, admit it. You spend a lot of time doing things you'd rather not be doing, things you do because you've always done them. Because somebody told you that's how they're done.

Ask yourself, "Is how I spend my time bringing me joy? Is it making my life bigger? If not, why in the heck am I still doing it?"

Maybe my daughter can't find her soccer uniform and the litter box needs to be changed and there's a sale on cat food at the Piggly Wiggly and I need to call my friend Ivy in Tucson and buy a birthday card for Bob's 64th birthday and there's a war in Syria and the looming threat of global warming and I need to quit eating so many Krispy Kremes, start drinking more water, remember to wear sunscreen. And did I mention the *Star Trek* DVD is overdue?

But I'm going to get out my screenplay and write just one sentence anyway.

~~~~~~~~~~~~~~~~

Just do it!

GENERATE THREE IDEAS
FOR SMARTPHONE APPS

*"To dare is to lose one's footing momentarily.
Not to dare is to lose oneself."*

— SØREN KIERKEGAARD, PHILOSOPHER

It's good to remember that at any moment, you are only one thought away from a million-dollar idea.

Joel Comm stumbled onto his with iFart, an app best described as a digital whoopee cushion. Last I checked, this silly app that features 26 choices of flatulence (Sneak Attack and Fart-a-Friend, to name a couple) had raked in a cool half million. It sold 113,885 units during its first two weeks alone.

I also spotted a Hello Cow app (poke it and it moos) and a voodoo app for uploading photos of your nemesis, complete with digital pins for placing a curse.

With more than a billion smartphones on the market, this is the week to crank up your idea machine, to put it to work inventing ideas for smartphone apps.

Zumba for the Soul

✺ Invite friends to watch the sunset. Hold up cards (1–10) to rate the "show."

✺ Celebrate the birthday of your favorite writer.

✺ Go to a movie dressed in costume.

You're in Good Company

Best-selling author Mary Karr described the running commentary in her brain when she writes: "F*ck. Sh*t. You dumb bitch—whoever told you that you could write?

WEEK 10

D.I.A.

"Adventures don't begin until you get into the forest. That first step is an act of faith."

— MICKEY HART, GRATEFUL DEAD DRUMMER

I might as well get it out now. I sometimes suffer from depression. I don't really like to admit it. I think it makes me sound weak. Inferior. At least a notch or two below Katy Perry.

When the big "D" tightens its ugly claws, I put on the boxing gloves and wage war. Unfortunately, it's always against myself.

"Well, Pam," is how it usually starts. "If you were really this vibrant, together person you claim to be, you could kickbox this thing out the door? Where's your willpower anyway?"

And then it goes downhill. "Who would ever want you? You're a disgrace, no good to anyone."

And then I get really mean.

A friend (perhaps I should say a former friend) once told me humans are meant to live from "glory to glory." My life pretty much moves from glory to darkness to glory again, which isn't too bad except when you're in the dark parts.

One therapist I consulted wrote my problem off with this comment: "Ah, you're a writer, a creative person"—as if it was a malady comparable to having an extra arm or a blinking antenna growing out of my head—"creative people just have these problems. There's really nothing you can do."

And for this I paid $120?

Luckily, I found out she was wrong. By complete accident, I discovered there *was* something I could do. It was 10 o'clock the night before a creativity class I was facilitating. I felt depressed. The class assignment—making a sculpture—was as appealing as a blind date with Ted Bundy. All I wanted was to get in bed and pull the covers over my head.

But I was the teacher. How could I rightly expect other participants to bring in a sculpture if I didn't? I wrestled with it for a while. I even started composing excuses for why I didn't get the project done. My computer developed a brain tumor. I couldn't drive because my garage door opener was broken.

There was this other voice, however, a beensy voice—as my daughter used to call tiny things—that kept trying to get through. It whispered something about D.I.A.

"What?" I asked suspiciously. "D.I.A.? What in the heck is that?

"Do it anyway!" the voice insisted.

Although I normally don't when I'm feeling like Sylvia Plath, I listened to this beensy voice. I decided to go ahead and attempt to tackle the project.

Somewhat reluctantly, I chose a picture of a girl jumping into the air for joy. She had on a peasant dress, her legs were bent, her arms spread wide, and her head was held high in ecstasy. In other words, she looked exactly the opposite of how I felt.

I copied this picture at several different sizes—50 percent, 100 percent, 200 percent. I cut the pictures out, applied cardboard and a Popsicle stick to each one, and mounted them, smallest to largest, on a cardboard tube. When I shone a light on the procession of happy, jumping girls, the one in the back made an even more impressive shadow on the wall behind it.

At about midnight, as I was packing up my sculpture for class the next day, it suddenly occurred to me that my depression had lifted. No, that is an understatement. I actually felt happy, enlivened, kind of like the girl in the picture.

What a revelation. For once, I didn't listen to the voice that told me I was much too tired and depressed to make a stupid sculpture, the voice that insisted the only rational plan of attack was to get in bed.

When you think about it, a voice that tells you you're worthless as dog doo-doo is not a voice you really want to heed.

The other voice, the one that can never be extinguished, thank God, is probably the one with my best interest at heart. And it told me to D.I.A.

For years, I kept this unique sculpture in my bedroom, not only because I liked the sheer bliss it represented, but because it reminded me I could break out of the grips of inertia, I could move through that hovering cloud of depression. I have a choice.

Not willpower, mind you. But choice.

It's pretty simple. Which voice are you going to listen to? The voice that says, "You? An artist? You flunked Miss Brightly's art class. You have as much talent as a tsetse fly."

Or the voice that says, "D.I.A."

It has become my motto. And it was as simple as a pair of scissors and a cardboard tube.

Just do it!

MAKE A SCULPTURE.

"You don't take baby steps for the distance they cover, but to put yourself within reach of life's magic."

— MIKE DOOLEY, MR. UNIVERSE HIMSELF

Any medium works. I once made a sculpture of George Washington from a used oatmeal container. Okay, so I was in fifth grade, but it was a sculpture nevertheless. Maybe you're ready for papier mâché, bronze, or a $1 bag of balloons and your own hot air. Up to you.

While balloon sculpting might sound frivolous, dig this. I recently met a husband-and-wife team who earns a respectable living making balloon sculptures at bars, festivals, and other special events. I watched them twist everything from Ariel, the Little Mermaid, to Elvis Presley, complete with black pompadour and gold lamé jumpsuit.

Zumba for the Soul

❀ Call the most creative person you know and find out what they're doing. It will inspire you.

❀ Learn two homeopathic remedies.

❀ Make six kinds of applesauce.

You're in Good Company

Nobel Prize winner Gabriel García Márquez, widely regarded as one of the 20th century's most significant authors, said, "All my life, I've been frightened at the moment I sit down to write.

GET DOWN
AND DIRTY

"The best way to complain is to make things."

— JAMES MURPHY, SINGER-SONGWRITER

This week, we're going to change our terminology. Forget creating art. Instead, we're going to "make stuff."

Here's why: Art has baggage. It's often pretentious and intimidating. It makes you stand up straight and mind your manners.

Consider most art museums. Not only are they huge structures with big columns and cavernous lobbies, but they're filled with stern guards who dress like policemen and dispense dirty looks. The art is sealed tightly behind glass. You can't get close enough to breathe on it, let alone touch it with your grubby little paws.

Art museums seem to set up a kind of "us" against "them" mentality. We're the peons who pay to look at art. The geniuses who create it are old guys from Europe who like to cut off their body parts.

And if there's anything 100 percent effective at bringing up unresolved insecurity issues, it's first-of-the-month Friday night art gallery openings. You have to dress really *cool*, preferably in something black, refrain from smiling, and, if at all possible, make your hair do something gymnastic. If you do say anything (my tack is stay mute, leading people to believe I'm deep in profound thought), it had better be brilliant. I always feel like an impostor.

That's why I like the idea of making stuff. It kicks pretense out the door. None of us in our fragile states as budding "stuff makers" need anything to do with approval. Forget Pauline Kael. Forget whether some snobbish art critic who only reviews art because he's too petrified to make his own likes it or not. We're simply making stuff. Every week, we're going to make something different—a poem, a song, a character.

Just remember it's only stuff.

My favorite art has always been made by what the art world calls folk artists or outside artists. Using whatever material is handy—tree trunks, old refrigerator doors, broken bottles—these poor, often rural folks just one day started whittling or stacking or painting. In other words, making stuff. Not only have few of them ever heard of Monet or van Gogh, but most of them have had little schooling of any kind.

Howard Finster, a retired Baptist minister who didn't pick up a paintbrush until he was in his 60s, had a 6th-grade education. One day, God said to him, "Howard, I want you to start painting." He quickly reminded God he had no clue how to paint and God retorted just as quickly, "How do you know?" That was 1973, and before he died in 2001, Finster had produced some 46,000 paintings. Of course, he also liked to paint accordions, lawn mowers, oxygen pumps, and telephones.

"Art?" you're wondering. Just ask Barbra Streisand, Woody Allen, and other fans who have paid upward of $20,000 for his artwork. Unpretentious? You bet. He produced all of his stuff from his vibrating bed in Summerville, Georgia.

In the old days, everybody made everything. If you wanted a new dress, you made it yourself. If the family dinner table wore out, you chopped down a tree and hauled it to the barn where the lathe and the wood shop was set up. There were no grocery stores or even if there had been, there weren't cars to take you there. You grew your own food, wove your own wall hangings, built your own house. Today, when someone says they built their own house, they mean that they bought blueprints from an architect they found online and hired craftsmen to "do the dirty work."

This is what we want to do: "the dirty work." It's what feeds us, what connects us to our true natures. When we let other people make all our things, we lose a piece of who we really are. We cut ourselves off from our source. By making things, we tap into a prolific wellspring that literally shapes us into masters.

Even those of us who cook our own food and weave our own wall hangings have turned over our Friday and Saturday night entertainment to the experts. We go to the movies or watch Netflix. It doesn't even occur to us to write our own scripts, sing our own songs. A hundred years ago there was no *Scandal* on Thursday nights, no *This Is Us* on Tuesdays, so if the family wanted to celebrate the end of a long day, they sat down and told stories or made up a song on the family guitar.

Art? Nah, they were just making stuff.

Just do it!

TRANSFORM SOMETHING
FROM A THRIFT SHOP

*"If you want to create or be anything bigger, better,
or truly different, you need room to ask 'What if'
without a conference call in 15 minutes."*

— TIM FERRISS, AUTHOR OF *THE 4-HOUR WORKWEEK*

Use paint. Or a saw. Or a sewing machine.

I used to buy old wooden chairs (average price: $5) and repaint them in vibrant southwest themes. Another time, I bought a bolt with 50 yards of heavy, white fabric, conned my mom into making dresses out of it, then went to work with the fabric paint. I love painting favorite slogans on my clothes—things like "Create or Die" or "Any time not spent on love is wasted."

Zumba for the Soul

❧ Have a board meeting with William Shakespeare, Nikola Tesla, and other dead creatives you admire.

❧ Come up with 20 uses for a pencil.

❧ Dye your hair a color you've never worn.

You're in Good Company

James Brooks won five Oscars for *Terms of Endearment*. You might think he'd have enjoyed the process. But, every day, he said, was sheer murder. "It was like walking into a propeller. I was always aware of how bad it might have been."

WEEK 12

ARTIST, HEAL THYSELF

"Here, when the danger to his will is greatest, art approaches as a saving sorcerer, expert at healing."

— FRIEDRICH NIETZSCHE, GERMAN PHILOSOPHER

Therapists spend years digging up issues that will surface immediately when you first attempt to paint or write. They're all there—unworthiness, the fear of not measuring up, the compulsion to eat a bag or two of barbecue potato chips.

Here you are painting a stupid still life of mangoes, and every single block that has ever prevented you from leading an exciting, fulfilling life shows up to air its laundry.

It's like *This Is Your Life*, the TV show where old friends and teachers show up to surprise and embarrass you.

"Hey, remember me?" the voices of shame and guilt call from backstage.

And you paid how much for a shrink to determine your major problem is thinking you're not good enough? Naming the problem, admitting that you eat or run or whatever it is you do when you're scared, is always the first step toward healing.

Notice I said the first step. It's always important to name a problem. I am an alcoholic. I suffer from depression. I was abused by my stepfather.

Just don't pitch a tent.

We read books about how powerful we are, do positive affirmations, paste little sticky notes to our bathroom mirrors, but we still get up every morning and repeat something like this:

"I am the adult child of alcoholic parents, the product of a dysfunctional family. I must be vigilant against my small self, the saboteur within which separates me from my good, and the ego that separates me from my God."

And the litany ends with something like, "But I am powerful."

What choice does your subconscious mind have but to say, *Bullsh*t?*

The mighty river of God flows through your soul, the infinite power of the universe pulses in your heart. And you want to be a survivor?

You are not your stuff. You are not your history. You have the power to heal, the power to make radical changes.

When you write a poem or sketch the new puppy born to the neighbor's Australian shepherd, you come to realize that you're more than the depression or the rheumatoid arthritis.

The act of creating taps the healing God-current that runs through all of us. It's the level that can't be reached through our pea-brain minds or our ego. It certainly can't be reached by looking at yourself in the mirror and affirming, "I am a survivor."

The act of creating drains away pay-the-rent, do-the-laundry details. It taps the deep subterranean impulse that recognizes magic and beckons us to wholeness. It repairs the defects.

Instead of telling everyone about your problems with your boyfriend—how he won't commit or how he falls asleep every night watching *Conan*—why not write a poem about it instead? The poem may just take you to the other side.

Performance artist Chris Wink put it like this: "Follow your muses instead of trying to solve the social wounds of your adolescence. We've lost a whole generation of people who are dealing with their environment by retreating, by going into therapy. So instead, you go to open mic at a crummy tavern and perform your art. Rather than being introspective and constantly working on your shortcomings, get angry, get excited, get social."

There is so much more inside you than you ever imagine. You fear you are shallow and little only because you won't or don't look.

Creating something gives you a voice.

Just do it!

MAKE A CREATIVITY VISION BOARD

"I've known for some time that staring at objects while holding pictures in my head makes reality oddly responsive."

— MARTHA BECK, AUTHOR OF *EXPECTING ADAM*

Martha Beck, who I met one year at an author's conference in Kansas City (we both had new books out), wrote an article for *O, The Oprah Magazine* about vision boards. As she said, "Some results are so successful that the hair on the nape of my neck prickled for months."

Anyone who has read *The Secret* (a group that includes pretty much everyone on the planet) knows about vision boards, where you cut out pictures of things you'd like to invite into your life for dinner.

However, this week, I'd like to talk about an even more important practice. Instead of making a vision board of things you'd like to receive, how about making one of things you'd like to give? Of things you'd like to create?

Use photographs, magazine cutouts, and anything else that jazzes you up about your creative projects.

Add a picture of yourself and add affirmations, quotations, and inspirational thoughts.

Zumba for the Soul

- ❦ Write five fortunes you'd like to find in a fortune cookie.
- ❦ Stage *The Newlywed Game* at home with three couples.
- ❦ Write five questions for *Trivial Pursuit*.

You're in Good Company

In the early '90s, George Clooney was being considered for the lead role in the homicide drama *Bodies of Evidence*. The CBS executive cast him instead as sidekick Ryan Walker after deciding Clooney was "just not leading man material."

INVASION OF THE BODY SNATCHERS

"It took 15 years to discover I had no talent for writing, but I couldn't give it up because, by then, I was too famous."

— ROBERT BENCHLEY, AMERICAN HUMORIST

Before the Renaissance and the age of rationalism, it was common knowledge that great artistry came from outside the artist. The ancient Greeks even had a name for these disembodied entities that body-snatched an artist. They called these outside forces "daimons," as in, "That Theophylaktos has been writing an awful lot of poetry lately. He must be bewitched by a daimon, lucky dog."

The going term in ancient Rome for this magical force that inhabited an artist was "genius," but it had a different meaning than the one we use today. A genius, to someone like Julius Caesar, was an attendant spirit, an unseen companion who delivered messages from the gods. Artists themselves weren't considered geniuses but merely vessels being put to use by this outside "thing."

Socrates believed he was tutored by a personal daimon. He considered it a divine gift and professed to blindly obey its every indication. In fact, he rarely did anything without consulting it, eventually even offering its guidance to all his friends.

Talk about a comfort. If the piece you're working on sucks, you can always blame it on the daimon or the inner genius. "Hey, I'm just the one taking dictation."

But then the Renaissance came along and the going construct became one in which the individual was placed at the center of everything. Forget things like magic and angels and disembodied beings delivering divine guidance.

Needless to say, the new construct hasn't worked all that well, having killed off hundreds of artists who couldn't live up to the pressure, stymying hundreds more who couldn't get started.

This week, we're going to take a U-turn back to the old construct, to the radical notion that invisible psychic forces are dying to help you with your creative projects. Some people call them muses. Some people call them angels or even God. The name doesn't matter. Asking for their help does.

Elizabeth Gilbert, author of *Eat, Pray, Love,* says this application to an outside force saved her during the writing of her now-famous memoir. She started invoking the "thing," as she calls it, on a particularly trying day. The work she was commissioned to write just wasn't flowing.

"I was in the pits of despair," she said. "I was having thoughts like *this is going to be the worst book ever written.*"

She even considered dumping the project, tried to figure out a way to repay the advance.

Suddenly, she remembered something Tom Waits told her. One day while driving on the L.A. freeway, a melody came to him. He liked it, would definitely have jotted it down. Unfortunately, with both hands on the steering wheel, he wasn't exactly predisposed for dictation. He yelled up at the "thing" and said, "Hey can't you see, I'm busy here. Go bother somebody else."

Gilbert decided she'd appeal to the outside voice, whatever it was. She looked up from the manuscript and hollered at the corner in her office: "Look, *thing*, you need to show up and do your part. I would like the record to reflect that I'm here for my part of the job. Where are you?"

That simple shift, moving from *her* doing the writing to letting the "thing" produce the manuscript gave us a memoir that has inspired millions.

Or consider Judd Apatow, who says anytime he writes something worth saying, he feels like he's channeling God.

"I don't write my stories—they write themselves," Ray Bradbury once told CNN. "A muse whispers in my ear and says, 'Do this. Do that.' I create these wonderful things out of my imagination and I look at them and say, 'My God, did I write that?'"

Just do it!

INVENT A NEW WORD

"Don't gobblefunk around with words."
— ROALD DAHL, AUTHOR OF *THE BFG*

In 1978, Robin Williams, playing Mork from the planet Ork, invented a new curse word: *shazbot*. Not only was it used in the show's opening credits, but it was eventually appropriated by *The Simpsons* (in the "Treehouse of Horror VI" episode), in the *Starsiege* video game, and by AC/DC singer Bon Scott, whose "shazbot, nanu nanu" became his last recorded words.

Shonda Rhimes, who was ordered by ABC's Broadcast Standards and Practices team to quit using the word *vagina* so often (never mind, that she could use *penis* 17 times with no recriminations), coined the term *vajayjay*, which is now part of modern lexicon.

What word are you going to add to tomorrow's dictionary?

Zumba for the Soul

- ❀ Plant a plant you've never heard of.
- ❀ Create a new daytime game show.
- ❀ Make a crossword puzzle.

You're in Good Company

After Harrison Ford's first small movie role, an executive called him into his office, shut the door, and informed him he'd never succeed in the movie business. Last I checked, his career has spanned six decades.

SECTION TWO

TAPPING THE DIVINE

"It is the vocation of the prophet to keep alive the ministry of imagination, to keep on conjuring and proposing alternative futures to the single one ordained by the king."

— WALTER BRUEGGEMANN,
OLD TESTAMENT SCHOLAR

Inside you are deep, wide, unfathomable dimensions. By serving any discipline of art you cast a rod into this bottomless mystery and bring up something that is normally beyond your reach. Someone described this "other" world as a stage magician's trunk. Although not apparent to the naked eye, the trunk has a trapdoor and secret drawers.

Art has transformational powers, not just for the individuals who practice them, but for society as a whole. Every time one person increases the voltage, all of us see more clearly.

To practice art, be it to chip a statue, arrange flowers, or write a situation comedy, is to affirm meaning, to say *yes* to the mystery despite all the tragedy and ambiguities that surround us.

There's a strong sentiment afoot that the arts are frosting—froufrou, expendable, unnecessary. This is the same voice that tells us we're expendable, the voice that assigns us a number, a punch card, a place in line.

The other voice, the magical voice, is the voice that calls us to be more. It's the voice of the universe.

As the following essays show, an artist is simply a prism that reflects God's light.

WEEK 14

"IT'S EVERYWHERE, IT'S EVERYWHERE."

*"The real power behind whatever success I have now
was something I found within myself—something
that's in all of us, I think, a little piece of
God just waiting to be discovered."*

— TINA TURNER, ROCK MUSICIAN

If you're like most people, you think of creativity as a private
club, reserved like the corner table by the window for a talented few. You believe it's passed out at birth to the Bachs, the
Matisses, the Michael Jacksons of the world.

You, on the other hand, (sigh!) are fated to be a con-
sumer of creativity, decorating your foyer with other people's
sculptures, spending your evenings watching other people's
visions on a 52-inch screen.

95

But the truth is all of us are creative. All of us are connected to a higher consciousness that allows us to see the glow so often blocked by low-flying clouds.

All of us have the ability to innovate, solve baffling problems, even produce art.

It's why we sing in the shower, write witticisms in the dirt on unwashed cars.

You were created in the image and likeness of the Big Creative Kahuna. Whatever your thoughts about God (and I know lots of us think of Him as a judgmental old toad who sits up in heaven salivating for the chance to mark down "naughty, naughty" in His big, black book), you can't really deny that a good percentage of the world agrees He'd probably include *creative* on His list of credentials.

Who else would bother to make every snowflake different? Every fingerprint on all 10 fingers of the world's 6 billion people unique? Even bugs, the lowliest of species, have been given great creative consideration. In the beetle family alone, there are more than 300,000 varieties.

Just like the barber who passes his razors down to his son, the Dude, as I call God in my book *E-Squared*, passed the ability to create down to us. Just like the engineer who smiles when his son builds a bridge out of his blocks, the Dude smiles when we write poems.

Most of us can accept that being like God means being kind, compassionate, giving canned corn to people less fortunate. But could it possibly also mean making a sculpture? The Big Guy, more than anything else, expects us to create, to express, to be more like Him. It is not only our right to create, but our responsibility and eventual destiny.

When you buy a smartphone, it comes with a host of apps—a calendar, maps, a camera, a calculator. Human beings, like smartphones, are also bundled with certain "software." We all come with the "app" to produce children, to think, to fall in love. Another program that's installed in every one of us is the creativity package.

At this point, it may be like iMovie on my iPhone, dormant and unused. But just like the purple starred icon in the right-hand corner of my phone, your creativity package is available awaiting your click.

When my daughter, Tasman, was five, she asked me, "Mom, do all tadpoles grow into frogs?"

I was stumped for a minute. Some of them probably don't. They get squished by a lawn mower, can't find enough flies, or run up against some other tadpole deterrent. But this I could tell her without hesitation—every single tadpole is encoded with the ability to "be a frog."

Might as well start ribbiting.

Just do it!

PREPARE AND TELL A JOKE

"Self-loathing never works."

— B. J. NOVAK, COMEDIAN, ACTOR, AUTHOR

Woody Allen wanted to be a magician until he discovered he could write one-liners for the New York tabloids. For 3 hours after school, he sat and wrote 3 or 4 typewritten pages with 50-some jokes.

So you never know where a good joke can lead you. My friend Todd started writing jokes—things like "a priest, a cowboy, and a quarterback walk into a bar"—and ended up touring the country as a stand-up comic.

Zumba for the Soul

- Invite someone you've never met to tea.

- Look through the want ads and find a job for which you're clearly not qualified, but might like if you were. Compose a cover letter, tell your future employer why you'd be perfect for the job. Stick it in the mail with your resume.

- Make a puzzle.

You're in Good Company

Thirteen publishers turned down William Kennedy's Pulitzer Prize–winning novel, *Ironweed*.

IMPORTANT CREATIVITY TEST

The SAT determines if you're bright enough for college, the LSAT tests law school potential, and the MCAT, which costs a whopping $310 every time you take it, predicts your affinity for med school.

But here, being offered for absolutely no charge, is the very best test I know for measuring creativity in human beings.

Get out your pencil.

PAM GROUT'S TEST OF CREATIVITY

1. Are you breathing?   Yes_____   No_____

Check your score here.

If you answered "yes" to the above question, you're highly creative.

WEEK 15

YOU SAY YOU WANT A REVOLUTION

"My destiny lies squarely on the back of my imagination."
— SHONDA RHIMES, CREATOR OF
GREY'S ANATOMY AND OTHER TV SHOWS

Those of you under 50 may not remember the physical fitness revolution. You may not remember life before the pump-it, dance-it, just-do-it days. Back then, it was not only acceptable to be a couch potato, it was really the only option.

The only people who "worked out" were professional athletes. The rest of us never considered the idea that we, too, needed physical exercise.

But then Dr. Kenneth Cooper coined the term *aerobics* and proposed the radical notion that everyone should exercise. Today, of course, there's not a Westerner alive who doesn't either engage in some sort of physical activity or feel guilty because he doesn't.

This same kind of revolution is happening with our brains—our creative muscle, if you will. It's not just professional artists who need creativity. Just as our bodies atrophy when we don't use them, so does our imagination.

Until we pry ourselves from our limited, habitual thinking, we will never solve the world's big problems. We will never find the wondrous world of connection, of magic, of true beauty that allows us to interact with the bigger thing.

When we curtail our vision to the rational world, the physical world, the world we experience through our five senses, we miss important things.

Imagination, on the other hand, can take you anywhere. It can write a story that can change someone's life. It can design a building, compose a song, inspire a nation.

It is my dream that *Art & Soul* will launch a revolution as big as the physical fitness revolution of the '60s. I envision office workers meeting over lunch hour to share poems. Friends making dates to write together in cafes, Saturday night paintfests where paper is taped to the wall, aprons are passed out, and people paint, not talk.

Already, there are pockets of people doing creative, satisfying, celebratory things.

In Lawrence, Kansas, where I live, people get up onstage and share true stories in what we call Story Slam. One guy might tell a hilarious tale about the Don Juan tree trimmer he hired. The next person might talk about her love affair with yoga. Those who don't share a story cheer and wage plans for next month when they'll be up there, strutting their stuff.

We all need to strut our stuff. That is why we were created.

So what if we're not in the pages of *People* magazine? Success, as far as I'm concerned, should be measured by pleasure, wholeness, and a sense of self-esteem.

Art is a tool for living, a spiritual calling. It doesn't matter who you are, how old you are, or where you come from. A creative life will lead you out into the wilderness, where life is raw, tangled, and rich.

A hundred years ago, we didn't need to jog or swim laps because most of us worked on farms, digging turnips and planting corn. We got enough aerobic exercise in day-to-day living. Likewise, our ancestors exercised their creativity in their day-to-day-lives. When they finished plowing the garden, they pulled out the family banjo and sang songs or they gathered around the hearth to tell stories. There was no such thing as 32-plex movie cinemas, Hulu, and Pandora.

This week, we're going to take back the reins of creativity. We don't need some publisher to tell us we're worthy of publication, some record producer to decide whether or not our songs are "up to contemporary American standards." Creativity belongs to all of us.

Just do it!

MAKE A SELF-PORTRAIT

*"I had the richly furnished and
impregnable keep of my imagination."*

— POE BALLANTINE, NOVELIST

When I made my self-portrait, I went to a photo booth where a couple bucks buys three poses. I went in with hats and different costumes (not that I had time to really change them between poses) and made faces.

I blew them up on a copy machine, added graphics and photos, and came up with, what I believe was, a unique self-portrait.

And remember: Frida Kahlo made a whole career out of painting nothing but her own self-portrait.

Zumba for the Soul

❀ Take your sketchbook to the park.

❀ Invent a toy you might have wanted as a kid.

❀ Send yourself a postcard.

You're in Good Company

Saul Bellow's college English professor dismissed him as "a dud." Bellow, who went on to write *The Adventures of Augie March* and *Humboldt's Gift*, ultimately won the Pulitzer Prize, the Nobel Prize for Literature, a Guggenheim Fellowship, and the National Medal of Arts. He is also the only writer to win the National Book Award for Fiction three separate times.

THE REAL GIFTS OF CREATIVITY

*"I want you to foam at the mouth
and wander into unknown fields."*

— NATALIE GOLDBERG,
AUTHOR OF *WRITING DOWN THE BONES*

Everybody from Eckhart Tolle to the graduate student leading a local mindfulness class insists that "being in the moment" is the key to happiness. I've tried meditating. I've tried yoga. I've tried reining in my fickle little mind that runs in 42 directions, but I still find myself thinking about the graduation party I'm supposed to be planning for my daughter, or the Visa bill that's due next Tuesday. In other words, something as elementary as "being in the moment" is not as simple as it sounds.

Finally, I've found something that forces me to be in the moment. It's called art, and the reason it works is because it's hard—make that impossible—to think about anything else when you're really immersed in painting or writing or whatever your art happens to be. Time literally hangs suspended. The run in my panty hose and the $80 speeding ticket I got last Thursday on my way to the dentist's office are the furthest thing from my mind. At times, it feels like touching the hem of the divine.

This is only one of the gifts creativity offers its disciples.

Most people have it wrong. They think the reason they want to write a book or a movie, to act, or to dance is because they want to be Matthew McConaughey or Joyce Carol Oates. They want to be on *Super Soul Sunday.*

They assume the fruit of creativity is seeing their name on the *New York Times* bestseller list or winning a gold statue named Oscar. Money, fame, and fans, they're sure, are the presents under the creativity Christmas tree.

Don't get me wrong. Those gifts are nice. And they certainly might come. Like Keith Richards of the Rolling Stones says, "People have the need to set people above themselves—like gods. I stand on the stage and I think, 'What are you looking at me for, a damned old junkie hacking away at the guitar?'"

Yes, many people make millions of dollars on their art. Sometimes, there's so much fame and so many fans that the only way to travel is incognito.

But that isn't the gift.

Fame has been described as a plate of cocaine. It certainly feels good for a while. It takes your mind off your everyday existence. But when it's all over (say in three weeks when you're bumped off the bestseller list by the next weight-loss book), you're crazy once again, searching desperately for that next fix, that next shot of fame.

Getting on a bestseller list does not a happy artist make. True gifts are those that rock lives, that shake things up and transform us. Getting a big advance might get you a new car or a ticket to the country club. But it won't crack open your heart or deepen your soul.

The real gifts will. The true gifts of creativity are the writing, the painting, the acting. The doing. It's the journey, always the journey, that bears fruit.

If you stick with your art, you'll be surprised at the freedom you will eventually gain. Serving an art fulfills our deepest needs to be heard, to be visible, to shout a holy "yes" to the miraculous.

Art opens our eyes, burns through the fog.

Serving an art prompts us to notice we live in a big world rich with details, abundant with beauty.

Once you start to recognize the drop of dew about to spill off the tip of the rose, the star shooting across the midnight sky, the dude with the green beanie who pushes his grocery cart to the bowling alley every afternoon, what step could be next but to say *thank you*?

Just do it!

START A DREAM JOURNAL

"Art is a collaboration between God and the artist, and the less the artist does the better."

— ANDRÉ GIDE, NOBEL PRIZE–WINNING AUTHOR

Put a notebook and pen beside your bed. This will help you identify recurring patterns, trends, and symbols and provide images and ideas for drawings and paintings and stories. It also alerts the muses that you're ready for their guidance.

Zumba for the Soul

- ⚘ Eat all your meals outside today.

- ⚘ Get up at 3 A.M. to see what's on television.

- ⚘ Go to a deserted field and dance.

You're in Good Company

Phil Collins was convinced his career was all dried up after releasing his debut solo album, *Face Value*, 11 days after his 30th birthday.

THE G WORD

*"We must accept that this creative pulse
within us is God's creative pulse itself."*

— JOSEPH CHILTON PEARCE, AUTHOR OF
THE CRACK IN THE COSMIC EGG

This is the week that may be hardest to swallow. The week where we consider the radical notion that God wants to help you with your creative projects, that He actually supports your wildest dreams.

I know what most of you think. That the higher forces or God, if you happen to like that word, live millions of miles away and are too busy working on world hunger to help you throw a pot or design a centerpiece. You can buy that God "moves mountains," but you can't fathom that He/She might also have some good thoughts for scene three in your screenplay.

Either that or we want to steer as far away from God as possible. After all, who wants to paint crucifixes or sketch portraits of the Last Supper? Drive those irrational thoughts from your head. God is about expanding, not about being stuck in little boxes with crosses, halos, and 10 commandments.

Early on, we put limits on God. We start to see Him as somebody like . . . oh, say . . . us.

The first step is to get over the God we made up. The God who is stingy and angry and wears a Led Zeppelin beard. We've got to consider the possibility that God actually likes us, that He's rooting for us to succeed.

Just who do you think it was that planted that dream in your heart, anyway?

God, in case you forgot, is the Great Creator. He was the first artist, the spark from which the rest of us come. Artists, after all, have a thing for other artists.

Why wouldn't God want you to create? Why wouldn't He want you to follow in His footsteps? He gave you the ability to dream and to create. Does He also have to give you the paintbrush?

Somewhere along the line, we picked up the preposterous notion that God's will for us has something to do with starving children in Africa, with wearing ashes on our heads.

Nothing could be further from the truth. God's will for you is complete and total happiness, and if you take a step in the direction of your dreams, She'll be right behind you with a host of heavenly cheerleaders, fist-bumping, high-fiving, and shouting, "You go, girl."

The Divine Source is as generous as you'll allow.

The Liars' Club, Mary Karr's memoir of her Gothic childhood in a swampy East Texas oil-refining town, won literary awards, sold half a million copies, and turned its then-40-year-old author, at the time an obscure poet, into a literary celebrity.

But it never would have happened, Karr admits, if it wasn't for "the bigger thing."

When she first reluctantly asked for help, she was a card-carrying cynic, only appealing to what she called "the subtle bastard" as a last resort and only because her AA sponsor insisted. Her initial reaction was, "No way . . . never gonna happen, no offense."

Even after she got a call from the Whiting Foundation, an endowment for emerging writers that awarded her a $35,000 prize she hadn't applied for, she held tight to her skepticism. It had to be coincidence that the call came within a week of asking the Big Guy for help, didn't it?

But the blessings started piling up. The more she requested guidance, the faster they came.

When she got the book contract for *The Liars' Club*, she was newly divorced, a single mom without a car.

"Hoping to get a book advance was like saying maybe I'll be an Olympic gymnast," she said.

Still, the call came, three days after handing her proposal to the literary agent she just *happened* to meet at a soiree she just *happened* to attend.

Today, Karr openly calls the invisible thing God and says she appeals to its guidance every day.

"I pray. I ask God what to write. I know that sounds insane, but I do," she says. "I have a sense that God wanted these books written. That doesn't mean they're meant to be bestsellers. But I do have a sense of being guided. Call it self-hypnosis, prayer, whatever. To skeptics I say, just try it. Pray every day for thirty days. See if your life gets better. What do you have to lose?"

Just do it!

PEN AN ELEVATOR PITCH
FOR A CREATIVE PROJECT

*"I will not wait another day to find
the treasure my Father offers me."*

— A COURSE IN MIRACLES

In Hollywood, movies are sometimes sold solely on a five-minute pitch. So come up with a concise, quick, alluring elevator pitch for either a movie or another creative project percolating in your brain.

Zumba for the Soul

- Eat four new fruits.
- Learn to yodel. Do it in a public place.
- Create a library of inspiring books.

You're in Good Company

Robin Williams was voted "least likely to succeed" in his high school class.

114

ART DIVINERS

*"You might as well fall flat on your face
as lean over too far backwards."*

— JAMES THURBER, AUTHOR

"Thank God, the public only sees the finished product."

— WOODY ALLEN, FILMMAKER

We idolize Picasso, enter radio contests to go backstage with
Bon Jovi, write fan mail to Leonardo DiCaprio, yet we don't
give the time of day to the Picassos and Bon Jovis within our
own homes.

That teenager at the Dairy Queen with the three screaming kids has a funny poem in her heart. The accountant
with the alligator briefcase has a rock video in his head. The

7-Eleven clerk with the purple hair has an original screenplay under the counter.

The people we walk by every day have untold talents, passions that beat in their chest like a witch doctor's drum.

But we're so busy watching the "real" artists on *Entertainment Tonight* that we don't even notice.

How many Barbra Streisands, Robert Motherwells, Laurence Oliviers do you already know? The guy you sleep next to every night, the woman who packs your lunch every morning have powerful yearnings and stories and songs. And yet, we yawn and ask if they've seen our brown socks. Instead of asking our loved ones to dance, we ask them to take out the trash.

Everywhere around us are people like John Suta, a 70-something retired pipe fitter from Eugene, Oregon, who despite heart problems and nerve damage in his legs, shows up every day with his tarnished French horn to practice with the Roosevelt Middle School band. People like Keith Anderson, a marketing manager from Westwood Hills, Kansas, who three times a week heads to a tiny workshop in his basement to blend fibers and dyes to make paper.

The call for magic beckons us like steam rising from a fresh-baked pie.

Yet, we still think Martin Scorsese, Mozart, and Julia Roberts are the ones who drew the lucky straws.

If professional artists did draw different straws, it's only that of being born in the right place at the right time.

If Mozart had not been born in 18th century Salzburg to a father who led the local orchestra, he might not have started composing.

If Matisse had been born in, oh, say, Sandusky, Ohio, it's unlikely he'd have become the artist he did. On the other hand, if Leroy Watkins had been born in Le Cateau-Cambrésis in 1869, his paintings might be seducing the big spenders today.

Renoir, Monet, Cézanne, Pissarro, Degas, and other Impressionists we now hail as geniuses became geniuses because they stoked those fires. They didn't ask, "Where are my brown socks?" They wanted to know how far they could go in capturing light and shadow, in recording the pleasures of their everyday lives. They became allies, sharing studio space and taking painting excursions together. They supported one another and nurtured this new "life-form."

Like the Impressionists, we have the power to make the place and time the right ones. We can stoke our genius, band together, nurture the art inside our brothers and sisters.

Wouldn't it be great to be able to say my town, Lawrence, Kansas, or Lewistown, Montana, was the birth of some new art form? And why couldn't it be?

Motown doesn't exist because all the musical talent was born in Detroit in the 1950s and '60s. It existed because one man decided to mine the talent that was there. He could have just as easily looked in Denver, Colorado.

Maybe the most important task any of us could undertake is to become a diviner of art, to take a willow switch and feel for the deep artistic vein that coils and creeps within our brothers, the vein that whispers, "You could be more."

Just do it!

BECOME AN EXPERT AT SOMETHING

*"You have to love your art because . . . you're going to get
married to it, you're going to go to graduate school
with it, sleep with it, fight with it, try to cut it out of
your life, and four or five years later, you'll endure
all those times and love it even more."*

— JEANINE TESORI, COMPOSER

Pick a topic and learn everything you can about it. Maybe
it's Tasmanian devils. Or growing herbs or coding computers.
The topic doesn't matter. Just make sure it's something that
inspires passion.

Zumba for the Soul

- Mime on a street corner.

- Go shopping in a Groucho Marx nose and glasses.

- Ride up and down in an elevator all day and draw shoes.

You're in Good Company

James Joyce couldn't start writing each morning until he smoked half a pack of cigarettes and consumed mass quantities of coffee. Finally, after all that, there was no further excuse.

WEEK 19

WR*I*TE YOUR OWN B*I*BLE

*"It takes courage to grow up and
turn out to be who you really are."*

— E. E. CUMMINGS, POET

My friend Greg Tamblyn, a talented songwriter, wrote a funny
song that became the title of his first album. It's called *The
Shootout at the I'm OK, You're OK Corral*. It starts like this:

> *I could tell that it was more than just a simple lover's spat*
>
> *When she called me compulsive and blamed my
> mom for that*
>
> *I yelled, "I'm not the only one with hang-ups gal"*
>
> *And thus began the shootout at the I'm OK, you're
> OK corral.*

It's funny because he and his girlfriend begin hurling insults at each other, lines they picked up from the latest self-help books. She says, "You've got the Peter Pan Syndrome. You never grew up." And he returns with, "Look who's talking? The Woman Who Loves Too Much."

It goes on to say:

I could tell she was going to fight me nail and tooth

When she brought up Dear Abby and quoted Dr. Ruth.

Although the song is hilarious, it touches a raw nerve. We're so busy quoting Dr. Ruth that we forget to quote ourselves.

What do we think?

Most of us have no idea.

We look outside for answers. We look to everybody except ourselves.

And it's a shame. Life is being wasted. We're not having the fun we could. We're not making the beautiful things we could. We're not living, not celebrating, not polishing the unique jewels each of us contains.

We're too busy cultivating the seven habits for highly effective people.

Why are we following rules that some author we've never met made up? I don't care how smart Suze Orman is, how together Joel Osteen is. They don't know the secrets to your life.

There's only one person who does.

What do you like? What is important to you?

Do you know?

An artist's first priority is to get acquainted with himself.

Only then can he sing his own song.

You must recognize in yourself an individual, someone who's very distinct from the others. Find the fine thing that you are. Only then will you be liberated.

Walt Whitman claimed nothing could be more enlightening than to have a frank talk with yourself. His one great battle cry was for each man to find himself and then to give evidence of this uniqueness to the world.

"*Leaves of Grass*," he wrote, "has been an attempt from first to last, to put a person, a human being (myself in the latter half of the 19th century in America) freely, fully and truly on record."

He encourages each person to write their own Bible.

After you do that, you should write your own prayer. Make up your own credo. Dance to your own piper.

Why are the vast majority of adults in this country bored, lonely, and afraid?

Because they don't know who they are.

There are gigantic things to be done—health care to be reformed, education to be improved. Most everything could be made more beautiful.

How could anyone be bored?

We could be creating out of thrilling delight. We should live each day in vibrant exuberance. Our only job on this great big planet is to find our vitality, to discover what makes us want to jump on the table and dance.

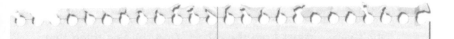

Just do it!

FORMULATE A SCENE
FOR YOUR NEW SCREENPLAY.

"Without your participation, art is only potential."
— DAVID BAYLES, PHOTOGRAPHER,
AUTHOR, AND WORKSHOP LEADER

What? You haven't started your screenplay? Okay, here's all you need to do. Make up a character. Put him or her in an elevator. Make up another character. He, too, steps in the elevator. Only problem is the elevator sticks between the third and fourth floors. What happens?

Zumba for the Soul

- Name an angel.
- Create a "drama." Ask Steve Harvey what to do.
- Design a birdhouse.

You're in Good Company

Abraham Lincoln, insecure about his 272-word Gettysburg Address, felt certain it would be quickly forgotten. After well-known orator Edward Everett praised the speech, Lincoln wrote back expressing gratitude to learn it had not been "a total failure."

WEEK 20

LISTENING TO YOUR OWN VOICE

"He was a bold man that first ate an oyster."

— JONATHAN SWIFT, AUTHOR OF
GULLIVER'S TRAVELS

When Walt Disney was in grade school, a well-meaning teacher peering over at the flowers he was scribbling in the margins of his paper tapped him on the shoulder and said, "Walt, honey, those flowers are nice, but flowers don't have faces."

Walt turned around, looked her straight in the eye, and pronounced boldly, "Mine do."

This is the confidence with which we must create.

We must refuse to listen to anything or anybody except the inner urgings of our soul. Very early on, we turn over the reins to something outside of ourselves. The coach tells us if we're good enough to be on the basketball team. The music teacher tells us if we have the talent to sing in the choir. Our teachers give us arbitrary grades that tell us if we're smart enough to make the honor roll, bright enough to get into college.

Our art teachers give us the rules: grass is green, skies are blue, and flowers do not have faces.

Robert Fulghum's now-famous essay "All I Really Need to Know I Learned in Kindergarten" was made into a stage play. In one of the first scenes, the kindergarten teacher asks her fresh young students how many of them are dancers.

"I am. I am," they all shout exuberantly.

"And how many of you are singers?" she continues.

Again, all of them wave their hands wildly.

"Painters?"

Unanimous hand-waving.

"Writers?"

More unanimous hand-waving.

In fourth grade, another teacher asks the same questions of the same students. Now, only a third of the students are dancers, singers, painters, writers.

By high school, the number who are willing to claim artistic talent is down to a paltry handful. Where did the confidence and enthusiasm go?

Some well-meaning parent or teacher probably told them they were not painters. Some aptitude test with a fancy title gave an official score that said they had better give up that misguided ambition to be a writer. Try accounting. Some guidance counselor broke the news that only a chosen few have artistic talent.

Why did we listen?

How can anybody else know what color your flowers are? How can anybody else know what notes you're supposed to sing?

In a book called *Musicians in Tune,* Jenny Boyd, former wife of Mick Fleetwood, interviewed 75 contemporary musicians—everyone from Eric Clapton to Branford Marsalis. She found many of today's successful musicians were outsiders, not part of the "in" crowd in high school. This alienation forced them to listen to that inner voice, the one that so often gets crowded out. Out of desperation and a sense of not belonging, they were forced to call up their own resources.

They held on to their power to decide whether or not their flowers had faces.

Throw off the shackles of those well-meaning parents, those misguided teachers. They know what's right for them. But they haven't a clue in Anchorage what is right for you.

Only you know that.

And you do know. You don't need another workshop, another book, another psychic reading. Bring it forth.

As for Walt Disney, well, his flowers certainly did have faces. In *Alice in Wonderland,* his 18th animated feature, the flowers not only had faces, but they had voices, opinions, and a chorus that entertained Alice with the whimsical song "All in the Golden Afternoon."

Just do it!

LEAVE YOUR PERSONAL STATEMENT SOMEWHERE.

"Graffiti is one of the few tools we all have. And even if you don't come up with a picture to cure world poverty you can make someone smile while they're having a piss."

— BANKSY, INFAMOUS STREET ARTIST

Yes, that means graffiti. Use a can of spray paint. Chalk will do. But the biggest part of this assignment is coming up with your statement. What do you need to tell the world? What do you know that needs to be said? Find a good place (the bus station, the sidewalk outside the grocery store) and go when no one is watching. And remember, a dusty car could be your medium.

Zumba for the Soul

🦋 Do a Polaroid study of mall rats.

🦋 Rent a Pink Panther video.

🦋 Eat two desserts naked.

You're in Good Company

Pulitzer Prize–winning poet Anne Sexton was too scared to take her first poetry class. A friend finally had to call and sign her up.

WEEK 21

GLORY TO GOD

"I was taught that prayer, like good manners, consisted of 'please' and 'thank you.'"

— ADRIANA DIAZ, AUTHOR OF
FREEING THE CREATIVE SPIRIT

"Now I lay me down to sleep . . ."

I must have droned that line 10,000 times.

Always the "good little girl," I rotely recited my prayers like a weedeater devouring hedges. Before meals, there was *God is great, God is good* . . . At bedtime, I prayed *the Lord my soul to keep.*

I might as well have been recanting the ABCs or reading the phone book. I felt no connection to God, no communion with the sacredness of life.

Instead of repeating a bunch of worn-out, has-been lines that somebody else made up, I should have jumped up on my bed and bounced my thanks to the Creator. I could have bounced "thank you" for the 32 fireflies I caught that night. Bounced "praise" for the purple Schwinn Billy Blotsky let me borrow. Bounced "sorry" for the naughty word I called my sister.

But no, it was the same old "now I lay me."

Jean Houston once wondered aloud if we're not boring God. Here He created this mind-boggling world with 25,000 species of orchids, lands as diverse as the Gobi Desert and Mount Fuji, and all we can do is mindlessly recite, "God is good, God is great."

When done properly, prayer is an act of spiritual intimacy, a profound expression of gratitude and respect. It opens us to Spirit's presence, lets us commune with something big and wide and brilliant.

In ancient cultures, art was always the mediator between man and God. Before priests convinced us we had to have a go-between, we interacted with God ourselves by prayerfully dancing, chanting, and making masks.

Still today, dervishes spin their prayers. African tribes drum theirs. Tibetan monks make mandalas. All are sacred acts, powerful methods for communing with the maker.

Kafka called writing his prayer. Jazz saxophonist John Coltrane prayed with his music, claimed it was the spiritual expression of his faith, his knowledge, his being.

Carlos Santana says it's impossible to separate his music from his spirituality.

"My music and intentions and energy and blessings all come from the same Universal Tone and I try to use them for the highest good," he says. "You have to stop taking this seriously and personally and getting all stiff, which only paralyzes your creativity and vitality. Find a human melody, then write a song about it. Make it all come through your music."

Art, whether it's cave paintings or toe-tapping gospel music, is a potent pathway to God. When done with the reverence and respect it deserves, it provides prophetic insight, magical moments of transcendence.

Try all you want, but years of religious study and "Now I lay me's" will never liberate you like true art.

Just do it!

INVENT A NEW BOARD GAME

"Come quickly, I am drinking the stars!"
— DOM PÉRIGNON, AFTER INVENTING CHAMPAGNE

Rob Angel was a waiter until he came up with the board game *Pictionary*, which sold 5 million copies in its first 6 months of national distribution. Maybe you want to make up a murder mystery game complete with characters who end up being suspects? A unique game that only your family plays? Invite your friends over and kick some ideas around.

Zumba for the Soul

- Practice a new walk.
- Perfect some animal noise.
- Tape paper to your TV and jot down ideas for your own TV shows.

You're in Good Company

Rodin failed three times to secure admittance to the École des Beaux-Arts in Paris. His uncle called him uneducable and his father said, "I have an idiot for a son."

ONCE UPON A TIME

> *"'You see, I don't know any stories.*
> *None of the lost boys know any stories.'*
> *'How perfectly awful,' Wendy said."*

— FROM *PETER PAN*, BY **J. M. BARRIE**

When my daughter was young, I read her a story every night before she went to sleep.

I started this sacred ritual while she was still in the womb, balancing such classics as *The Secret Garden* and *The Prince and the Pauper* on my growing belly.

When she was three, she started asking for stories that weren't in books—stories about when she was a baby, tales from my childhood, sagas from her heritage.

"Tell me the one with the pages inside you," she said one night.

She wanted to understand where she came from, how she fit into the big picture. She wanted me to tell her a story from my heart. I cleared my throat and began . . .

The Kalahari bushmen believe that a man's story is his most sacred possession. They know something we've forgotten. Without a story, you haven't got a country or a culture or a civilization.

One of actor James Woods's prized possessions is the canvas bag he used to deliver newspapers when he was a boy. A few years ago, his mother returned it to him with a note pinned to it. The note said, "Never forget where you came from. It will hold you in good stead."

Knowing and telling where you came from will indeed keep you in good stead.

When we fail to tell our story, we lose a part of ourselves. When we keep quiet, don't tell, we lose our footing.

Our stories liberate us. When we're able to tell our story we feel alive. That's why new love feels so glorious. We've got an audience for our story, a brand new person who hasn't yet heard endless recounting of our joys and our sorrows. It's not that we're so smitten with this other person. We're smitten with ourselves, with the unique person our stories are about. When love goes stale, it's often because we've quit telling stories.

Stories connect us to ourselves and to one another.

In 400 BC, Socrates was upset by the new fad—writing—because it threatened the storyteller's tradition. He declared: "The discovery of the alphabet will create forgetfulness in the learners' souls because they will not use their memories."

It's probably a good thing he never heard about Dish Network and the Internet.

When we're entertained by TV with its constant noise and instant gratification, we're not called on to use our imaginations, to interact, or to react. We just lie there, numb and mindless.

We've done exactly what Socrates feared—we've lost our memories, forgotten our stories, turned away from the very thing that binds us together in our humanity.

Artists are today's storytellers. Whether their stories are told in paintings, in films, or in bedtime reveries, artists keep the history of their tribe. They pass down traditions, define the time in which they live.

Don't you have a story to tell?

Just do it

PLANT YOUR FAMILY TREE

*"I think what the American family
needs is more dancing, don't y'all?"*

— VIVI FROM *DIVINE SECRETS
OF THE YA-YA SISTERHOOD*

What do you know about the country from which your family
hails? How did they get from there to here? Do you know the
story of your ancestors? If possible, plan a trip to your heritage
homeland. Perhaps you still have distant cousins there.

Channel Alex Haley, who became a household name
when he sat down and dug up his family tree. Your roots are
just as interesting. *How to Trace Your Family Tree* by the American Genealogy Research Institute might help.

ONCE UPON A TIME

Zumba for the Soul

- 🎵 Do a rain dance.

- 🎵 Write a new Facebook profile.

- 🎵 Stage a poetry reading around a campfire.

You're in Good Company

In a writing program at Stanford, classmates Thomas McGuane, Larry McMurtry, and Ken Kesey were not even remotely the best writers.

SECTION 3

KILL BILL

WHERE WE EXACT REVENGE UPON THE MANY MYTHS ABOUT CREATIVITY

"I was just a girl who held her heart in her hands and then tossed it out for all to see."

— JEN LEE, FILMMAKER

Just like Beatrix Kiddo, masterfully performed by Uma Thurman, who hacked up her enemies in the Quentin Tarantino classic *Kill Bill*, this section is meant to put a samurai sword through the countless whoppers that have been perpetuated in the name of art and creativity for the last several centuries.

As did the Bride, we're finally waking up from our coma. And, baby, the following essays will stab to death those nasty b*tches who have kept us from being who we are: kick-ass creators with countless gifts, stories, and inspiration to shake up the world.

MYTH #1: TO MAKE ART, YOU NEED MONEY

"I cannot afford to waste my time making money."

— JEAN LOUIS RODOLPHE AGASSIZ,
SWISS-AMERICAN BIOLOGIST

I am forever grateful I never ran across the famous French novel *Scènes de la vie de Bohème* by Henri Murger.

I'd have probably loved the novel that was wildly popular in the mid-19th century. Revolving around a group of impoverished artists who lived in the bohemian quarter of Paris, this bestseller spawned Giacomo Puccini's 1895 opera *La Bohème* and is widely credited as being the catalyst for the now-household term *starving artist*. Like Rocky and

Bullwinkle, pancakes and syrup, the words *starving* and *artist* have been joined at the hip ever since. How many posters have you seen for starving artist shows or starving artist sales?

But it's an exceedingly dangerous belief for any artist to subscribe. And it's the first of our list to meet the chopping block. Using these words, even as a joke, perpetuates an energy field that does none of us any good. It cements an antiquated belief that (a) you can't make art without money (so untrue, it's preposterous), and (b) if you're an artist, you'll always be broke.

Luckily for me, I didn't buy either maxim.

I was naïve enough to believe I could make a living as a writer. Without a trust fund. Without a bunch of savings in the bank. Without really anything but my own fool imagination.

You might have noticed my last name is not Rockefeller. Not only did I grow up with a glaring lack of silver spoons, but my father was a poorly paid Methodist minister in a tiny town in Kansas.

It was very clear to me that if I was going to reach my dream of being an author, of inspiring the masses with my words, I would have to rely on a different kind of capital. I would have to amass creative capital.

This unique retirement plan has been my saving grace, especially since I didn't fare exceptionally well in the ranks of corporate America. Even after securing a college degree, my one concession to the normal paradigm, I bristled at thoughts of a "real job."

Even a semicorporate job (a theme park that, at the time, was owned by Lamar Hunt, the guy who owned the Kansas City Chiefs) frowned on my choice of footwear and my "let's throw it out there and see what happens" attitude.

I've never felt the need for surveys, market research, and prescribed plans that, sure, might work for some, but offer no guarantees for me. I prefer traipsing to the well of the unknown, the river of infinite potentiality, the field of the brand-new.

That's not to say I always believed in myself. That would be like saying van Gogh didn't suffer mental illness.

But between bouts of lying in bed and staring at my ceiling fan, I found the wherewithal to believe I could create work that someone might enjoy. Between thoughts of unworthiness and self-pity, I believed I could devise creative capital with nothing but a good idea.

I was able to self-publish not one, but two books. I put them out there even though I was a single mom with a three-year-old (for the first one) and a seven-year-old (during the production of the second one).

It's one thing to call myself a freelance writer when it was just me, sharing homes with friends, trotting around the globe. But when I became a parent, it was expected I would settle down, be realistic, get a real job.

I am very grateful I didn't listen to the conventional paradigm.

Because here's the thing. You don't need money to be an artist. You need but one thing. Persistence to keep getting up off the floor where you sometimes lie (or at least I did) with your face pressed against the cold concrete, moaning, "What was I thinking?" You just keep getting up and taking the next step.

When you have no budget, you're forced to get creative. You *have* to find new and interesting ways to get things done. Like collaborating with others, like trading services.

I would never argue it's not easier with money. Yoko Ono might not be considered one of the pioneers of interactive art if her maternal grandfather hadn't founded Japan's massively successful Yasuda Bank. Or Rachel Rose, whose *Everything and*

More video might never have made it to the Whitney in 2015 if she hadn't hailed from one of New York's most powerful real estate fortunes.

But there are thousands of exceptions—like filmmaker Robert Rodriguez. He grew up in a family of 10 kids. If he had bought the myth about money, he wouldn't be the successful moviemaker he is today.

He raised the money for his first film by volunteering as a test subject for experimental cholesterol drugs. During the 30 days he spent in the lab, being subjected to who knows what kinds of side effects, he managed to write the script for *El Mariachi*.

He was 22, a new college graduate, and the Spanish-language *Mariachi* was a follow-up to the 8-minute film he made with a wind-up camera he secured at a thrift store. Called *Bedhead*, it fared quite well on the festival circuit even though it cost a measly $800.

As an experiment, he decided his next project would be a full-length feature . . . just for practice, just because it sounded fun.

"I figured if I could make an eight-minute film for eight hundred dollars, I could make a hundred-minute feature for eight thousand. And if I did everything myself (the financing, the writing, the editing, the lighting, the casting), I'd get as much experience as I would in film school."

So he called his cousin in Mexico who had a ranch where the bad guy could live and a friend with a bar where the shoot-out could take place. Another friend had a pit bull, yet another had a turtle, so they, too, were cast.

"I did not expect anyone to see this film," Rodriguez says. "It was done purely as an exercise in creativity."

In fact, when the Spanish, subtitled film went to Sundance and won the prestigious audience award, he felt the need to explain that it was meant to be a demo, a showpiece for his portfolio.

"See that Columbia logo at the beginning of the film?" he asked the audience. By then, he had sold it to a studio. "It cost more than the whole film."

Money offers a leg up, but it's far from imperative.

Just do it!

MAKE A YOUTUBE VIDEO

*"Money was never the goal; it was freedom.
I just wanted to be able to not go to work."*

— SHAY CARL, YOUTUBE SUPERSTAR

This week, you're going to be a filmmaker. Joel and Ethan Coen started with a Super 8 camera, which they used to recreate movies they saw on TV. In junior high, they made their big leap, moving from copycat to creating their own films. *Henry Kissinger, Man on the Go,* starring 11-year-old Ethan in a suit carrying a briefcase, was filmed at the Minneapolis–Saint Paul International Airport.

The Academy Award–winning duo say their movies now (*The Big Lebowski, Fargo, No Country for Old Men*) aren't all that different.

Or consider Shay Carl Butler, who went from feeding his family of five kids on food stamps to being a YouTube millionaire. His Shaytards channel (named after his first video of him prancing around in his wife's unitard) has some 3.5 million subscribers. Although Shay Carl just announced he was retiring for at least a year, the videos of his family's silly antics have allowed him to buy a huge ranch in Idaho; land endorsement deals with Target; meet the likes of Matt Damon, Dave Ramsey, and Steven Spielberg; and create a channel (along with other YouTube stars) that sold to Disney for nearly $1 billion.

All you need? A smartphone. The YouTube video editor (free on YouTube). And the ability to press record.

Zumba for the Soul

- Host a full-moon ceremony.
- Create the perfect boyfriend for Mindy Lahiri of *The Mindy Project*.
- Write down every good thing anyone has ever said about you.

You're in Good Company

Ludwig van Beethoven was incredibly awkward on the violin and was told by his teachers that he didn't stand a chance in hell at succeeding in composition.

MYTH #2: TO MAKE ART, YOU NEED THE APPROVAL OF A PUBLISHER, A RECORDING COMPANY, AN ART GALLERY, ETC.

"You no longer have to wait for the gods of corporate America or the university or the media or the investor to come down from the clouds and choose you for success."

— JAMES ALTUCHER, AUTHOR OF *CHOOSE YOURSELF*

New Thought leader Mary Morrissey tells a funny story about celebrating the holidays in Cabo. On the last day of her family vacation, her grown kids decided to rent individual ATVs to navigate the dunes and beaches. Mary pled supreme contentment and utter satisfaction in an effort to get out of it.

"I'm happy just to sit up here and watch," she said.

But finally, the kids shamed her into joining them. It even proved to be kind of fun until she got stuck at the bottom of one of the dunes. Her kids, one by one, came down to give her encouragement, all to no avail. She'd rev up her vehicle, get halfway up. They'd all be cheering, but, alas, she'd slide back down.

Finally, her son-in-law came down, noticed she was riding the accelerator and the brake at the same time.

"Mammi," he said. "You have power you're not using."

And that's this week's theme. The power to create lies, not at the nod of an editor or a producer or an agent. It lies in three simple letters: *DIY.*

I have managed to etch out a pretty awesome career on what amounts to a micro-budget. For many years, my company, if you want to call it that, was a one-woman show. My tiny, back bedroom publishing company, Patootie Press, published two successful books, no vetted publisher in sight. This was long before Amazon and Kindles and the numerous self-publishing platforms today that make self-publishing so much easier.

To this day, I still do my own social media, my own correspondence, my own bookings, and my own research, which, as I explained earlier, usually amounts to whatever the muses decide to whisper in my ear.

For *Jumpstart Your Metabolism*, my first effort (it was later sold to Simon & Schuster), I not only wrote the book, but I designed the cover, typeset the interior, and drew and painted the scales on the cover. Taz and I together drew the cartoons for the cover of *Recycle This Book,* the book I self-published in 2002, on brown paper grocery bags.

There's an unmistakable edge in not having to wait to hear back from your editor, your agent, your publicist. I managed to get *Recycle* out, even landing segments on several local TV shows in time for Earth Day, despite having come up with the idea a few shorts months earlier.

Or take Ani DiFranco, who has released more than 20 albums on her own independent label, Righteous Babe.

"It wasn't like I opened a big office in downtown L.A. with a staff of hundreds and a big blinking sign," she says. "It was really more like I made a little recording, a very humble recording, direct to tape—very cheap—to sell at my gigs in bars."

When you give up your need to be chosen by the experts, the so-called professionals, no one has power over you. You get to make your own way. Protect your own vision. Live freely in service to the creative spirit.

Just do it!

COME UP WITH THE TITLE AND SUBJECT FOR YOUR TED TALK

"We live in an era where the best way to make a dent on the world may no longer be to write a letter to the editor or publish a book. It may be simply to stand up and say something . . . because both the words and the passion with which they are delivered can now spread across the world at warp speed."

— CHRIS ANDERSON, OFFICIAL TED TALK CURATOR

As you may know, TED is a global community devoted to spreading good ideas. The short, 18-minute-or-less TED Talks cover everything from science to business to global issues. The original TED Conference, held annually in Monterey, California, brings together inspired thinkers whose good ideas hopefully open minds, spark conversation, and change the world. This week, you're going to add your voice to this clearinghouse of free ideas.

What is your one idea that can change the world?

1. Pick an idea that makes your heart race, that you know something about in a way that no one else does.

2. Connect your own story. A TED Talk is an idea made human through you.

3. Pass something on that will get people talking.

And while I'm not making any promises, a good TED Talk can scale up your visibility. After Brené Brown's evocative TED Talk on vulnerability was uploaded to the TED.com site, the little-known professor got 11 million views, an appearance on Oprah, and 6-figure book deals.

Zumba for the Soul

- Write the acceptance speech for your Oscar.
- Design a logo.
- Have "hat night" at dinner.

You're in Good Company

After Fred Astaire's first screen test, the memo from the testing director of MGM said: *Can't act. Slightly bald, can dance a little.* Astaire hung that 1933 memo over the fireplace in his Beverly Hills home.

WEEK 25

MYTH #3:
DOING ART ISN'T
A REAL JOB

"Growing up is highly overrated. Just be an author."

— NEIL GAIMAN, AUTHOR

In grade school, it's perfectly acceptable to answer the question "What do you want to be when you grow up?' with something like ballerina or rock star.

Our interrogators giggle, think it's cute. But by the time we're in high school, the answer to that ubiquitous question had better revolve around something practical, something that involves white (or blue) collars, computers, and paychecks.

I can't tell you how many times I've heard some variation of this question:

"When are you going to grow up, get a real job, quit f*cking around?"

In other words, most people think: *Being an artist is not a real job.*

Most of us catch very few glimpses of real working artists except on TV, and everybody knows that people on TV are way different than you or me.

Performance artist Amanda Palmer said until she was 11 and attended a live concert, she had no idea that artists like Cyndi Lauper, Prince, and Madonna were real people.

"I thought they were being convincingly played by actors," she says.

In her book *The Art of Asking*, Palmer details story after story where she wasn't taken seriously as an artist.

Even though she was making an ample living working as a living statue in Harvard Square, she often felt defensive and took it personally when people drove by, flipped her the finger, and yelled, "Get a job."

As she says, "This *was* my job."

"I mean, sure, it's a weird job. A job I'd created out of thin air with no permission from a higher authority. But I was working and people were paying me. I was making a consistent income. Didn't that make it a job?"

Even worse than the finger flippers was the voice in her own head, the voice she nicknamed the fraud police.

It went something like this.

"What makes you think you deserve to earn money playing your little songs?"

"What give you the right to think people should give one sh*t about your art?"

"When are you going to be a productive member of society?"

After years of battling her inner fraud police, she finally came to the realization that changed her life: you're an artist when you say you are.

"Going to art school, getting a publisher, getting signed is all bullsh*t. Whether or not you're an artist is in your head."

Only you can vote yourself off the island.

Just do it!

CREATE A COSTUME

*"My goal is to say or do at least
one outrageous thing every week."*

— MAGGIE KUHN, FOUNDER OF THE GRAY PANTHERS

Patch Adams, the rebellious doctor immortalized in the 1998 movie starring Robin Williams, says he can't conceive of practicing medicine without creativity, insists art is every bit as essential to diagnosis and treatment as the surgical suite. Without art, he says, life is sterile and meaningless.

Patch believes in injecting surprise, fun, and outrageousness into each day. Most days he wears a clown suit. He also owns a gorilla costume. And a ballet tutu. He gives himself exercises to do—like call 50 names in the phone book and practice making conversation.

Great freedom comes in taking risks, stepping outside the tiny line society prescribes as "normal." He suggests making an ass out of yourself every day—until it no longer feels uncomfortable. Start with what Patch calls "ridiculous raiment," clothes that are loud, bright, and clash. Given the narrowness of fashion standards, it's not difficult to come up with something to provoke chuckles and remind people there are limitless possibilities. Patch recommends fire hats, space helmets, and beanies with whirring propellers.

Zumba for the Soul

- ℳ Dress up like Elvis. Go dancing.

- ℳ Stage a watermelon-seed spitting competition.

- ℳ Dye socks and a T-shirt to match.

You're in Good Company

Meryl Streep, who has been nominated for more Academy Awards than anyone in history, was rejected for the main female role in *King Kong* because Dino De Laurentiis thought she was "too ugly."

"This was a pivotal moment for me. This one rogue opinion could derail my dreams of becoming an actress or force me to pull myself up by the bootstraps and believe in myself. I took a deep breath and said, 'I'm sorry you think I'm too ugly for your film, but you're just one opinion in a sea of thousands and I'm off to find a kinder tide.'"

MYTH #1: REAL ARTISTS HAVE LEARNED TO "DO IT RIGHT" IN ART SCHOOL

"Expertise is the enemy of imagination."

— ALEKSANDAR HEMON, AUTHOR OF
NOWHERE MAN AND *THE LAZARUS PROJECT*

Let's get the uncomfortable news out of the way. The world as we know it is toast. Nearly everything we have counted on, invested in, believed in is, for all practical purposes, over.

Corporations are dying, the middle class is shrinking, educational costs are skyrocketing and even those who do manage to get the Golden Fleece of a college degree have little guarantee of much of anything. Every aspect of our lives is in the process of transformation.

To rely on the old life plan (go to college, learn to do something, and then spend a lifetime doing it) is turning out to be hazardous to your career. No matter what some politician promises, no matter how much you invest in your 401(k), all guarantees, all bets are off.

In the virtual blink of an eye, the dominant economic system in the Western world has ceased to be a reliable teat on which to suckle.

There's no question capitalism worked for a long time. It produced massive amounts of wealth, lifted hundreds of millions out of poverty, and educated billions. Before technology and globalization, the American Dream, a term coined by Fannie Mae to convince two-income, post–World War II families to take out mortgages, had a compelling résumé. There were jobs out the wazoo. American industrialization spread throughout the world.

But what most of us failed to recognize is that the American Dream, decked out in the costume of million-dollar marketing slogans, had a Dr. Jekyll lurking in the back closet.

Created by a few select institutions that enslaved us with the preposterous notion that we're happier when we consume, that if we work really, really, really hard at their agendas, we'll be rewarded with weekends and vacations and a white picket fence, the American dream is caving in.

"Everyone I knew hated their job and was living in pain," author davidji once told me about his stint on Wall Street, before he quit to teach meditation. "It's as if our culture has perfected the art of making people feel unnecessary."

Anthropologist David Graeber echoes davidji: "It's a scar across our collective soul that huge swathes of people, in Europe and North America in particular, spend their entire working lives performing tasks they secretly believe do not really need to be performed. The moral and spiritual damage that comes from this situation is profound."

I'm happy to announce that the prison gates are now officially open.

Which is why this is such an exciting time. Our culture is in the process of being rearranged.

Thanks to the democratization of digital technology, anyone who wants to can follow his or her dreams. The tools are now available for all of us to be innovators, artists, inventors, creators.

We live in a time when one person writing at the coffee shop on her computer can reach millions. We live in an era when anyone who wants has leverage and a platform.

By the sheer good fortune of being human, you have all the tools, all the resources you could ever need to create an insanely meaningful, productive, and prosperous life.

Each one of us has inner assets and a connection to a spiritual realm, a higher vision that knows how to craft a new world, a world that works for all of us. These unseen forces have been waiting for a very long time for us to ditch the obsolete notion that there are rules and that we need to learn from human "experts."

It is time to put our faith, our hearts, and our treasures in *our* dreams and visions. Not the schemes and vision of *the Man*.

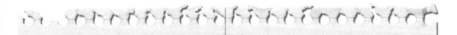

Just do it!

GENERATE 10 BUSINESSES
YOU COULD START FROM HOME

"They say when opportunity knocks you should let it in and invite it to sit at your table. F*ck that—when opportunity knocks, you should take it captive. I've got opportunity tied to a chair in my basement with a ball gag in its mouth. If you keep quiet, you'll hear it whining."

— TRACY MORGAN, COMEDIAN

Remember the guidelines? You don't have to start them. They don't have to be good. Repeat after me: I'm simply stretching my idea muscle. It's yoga for the imagination.

Zumba for the Soul

- ❧ Write a fan letter to yourself.

- ❧ Come up with five new outrageous affirmations.

- ❧ Pretend to be your favorite actress or actor today.

You're in Good Company

Ten-time Grammy award winner Bonnie Raitt says, "It's terrifying coming up with something new. I think too much and judge too much."

MYTH #5: TRUE ARTISTS ARE GENIUSES

"Down on the corner was a song, waiting to see if anyone would hear it."

— NATIVE ELDER AT THE WARM SPRINGS INDIAN RESERVATION

I once gave a workshop in Japan to 1,600 screaming fans, many of whom met me at the Tokyo Narita International Airport wearing a facsimile of my face on their heads. This exuberant fan club also brought a huge banner, dozens of gifts, and a piñata-like device that released hundreds of yellow paper butterflies, a sign I mentioned in my book *E-Squared*.

During my entire week in Japan, people shrieked when they saw me, begged for my autograph, and treated me as if I was some kind of VIP. As I told my possibility posse when I returned home, I felt like the Beatles.

But what these Japanese fans don't realize is the books they love, the books with my name on them, are only partly my doing. Every book I've ever written is far more brilliant, far more perceptive, and far more interesting than this creaky-boned person named Pam Grout. When I need a pep talk, it's not uncommon to get out my own books to reflect on my own words.

The creative projects with which we're entrusted are living entities with their own wisdom. We must acknowledge them as real things. We must recognize they are much smarter than we are.

Our job is but to shake hands and invite them in.

Pablo Neruda, the Nobel Prize–winning poet, claims words that were not his walked into his life from an unknown source. Poetry found him.

To give birth to your creative ideas is more of a yielding.

In her book *Big Magic*, Elizabeth Gilbert tells the story of a creative project that came knocking after *Eat, Pray, Love*. The story centered around a middle-aged spinster named Evelyn, who, after 25 years of being in love with her boss, was sent to the Brazilian rainforest to investigate the company's investment in a highway project that disappeared.

"It felt epic and thrilling," she said, a sure giveaway it was a story to which she could commit. She began ordering books about Brazil, studying Portuguese, turning down social invitations so she could work on her new project. She wrote a proposal, got a book deal. But then "a real life drama" derailed her.

After Felipe, the lover-turned-husband she met in Bali was refused entry into the United States, she put her notes into storage and flew halfway around the world to be with him.

By the time they worked through all the immigration issues and were finally able to return to the States, two years had passed. And as she says, "That was a long time to leave an idea unattended."

When she finally got out her notes, eager to begin, she discovered that, alas, her novel had taken leave. The juice was gone.

That could have been the end of it, but two years later, in 2008, she met novelist Ann Patchett. After serving together on a panel, they became friends, started exchanging letters, and Ann casually mentioned she was writing a novel about the Amazon.

Elizabeth was eager to hear more, since, after all, she, too, had once been invited by the muses to delve into the Amazon.

They were sitting at breakfast when Ann said to Elizabeth, "Okay, you go first. Tell me your Amazon story."

Elizabeth summarized her ex-novel as succinctly as possible. Ann stared at her as if she'd just said she was going to order a side of babies to accompany her bacon. She literally sat there mute for a full minute, after which time she finally said, "You have got to be f*cking kidding me."

Ann's novel, which by that time she was feverishly working on, was about a spinster from Minnesota in love with her boss who gets involved in a harebrained business scheme in the Amazon jungle. Money and people go missing, and her character is sent to Brazil to solve the mystery, at which point her quiet life is completely turned into chaos.

It took them a while to regain their composure, but they soon deduced that the idea, tired of waiting around for

Elizabeth, decided to find someone else who was available to midwife it into existence.

When the idea pops out of the jack-in-the box, it's show-time. It's time to commit.

I'll end with this funny observation from Robert Rodriguez, who never fails to credit his impressive output and creativity to the unknown mystery. "I can just picture the muses looking down on us, shaking their heads and tsk-tsking, 'Well, that bastard took credit for it again.'"

Just do it

COMPOSE A "THIS I BELIEVE" ESSAY

"I was always thinking, always writing, always sensing something in the soil that's about to emerge."
— LIN-MANUEL MIRANDA, CREATOR OF *HAMILTON*

From 1951 to 1955, CBS Radio Network aired a popular show called *This I Believe*. Hosted by Edward R. Murrow, the show encouraged both famous and everyday people to write short essays about their personal motivation and philosophy on life and to read them on-air. A print version was syndicated to 85 newspapers across the country.

NPR took up the mantle in 2005, and it's still going strong today. Several universities introduce it to incoming freshman, use it in English class, and encourage students to hone their "why?" as a way of tapping into their core values. As University of New Orleans writing teacher Ali Arnold once said, "When you tap into the essential . . . you can reach higher."

This week, you'll write your own version of *This I Believe*.

Zumba for the Soul

- Make a papier-mâché piñata.

- Paint a picture on a brown paper grocery bag.

- Decorate a bicycle.

You're in Good Company

Three years after *The Great Gatsby* was published, F. Scott Fitzgerald had only earned $5.15 in royalties. By the time he died, it was out of print.

MYTH #6: ARTISTS ARE MUCH MORE TALENTED THAN ME: WHERE WE FURTHER DEMYSTIFY THE ARTIST

"I was just a pawn with a pen, taking it all down."

— SUSAN G. WOOLDRIDGE, POET

Natalie Goldberg, poet, painter, Zen Buddhist, and author of *Writing Down the Bones*, one of my favorite books on writing, was once asked about talent. She said, "I guess I don't believe in talent. I know talent exists. Like maybe you're born pretty— but so what? What does that get you?"

Talent is like an underwater stream—equally available to everyone. You tap into it with your effort, and it flows through you.

When someone decides to dig for oil, nobody questions whether or not they have the "proper talent." The oil is there. It isn't thinking, *Well, I like those Koch brothers more than Pam Grout.* It's there for anybody who has the desire to keep digging. Nobody needs to see your degree, nobody cares if you have formal training.

Granted, some of us live in Russia or Texas or Saudi Arabia, where every other acre has a potential oil well, but what's to stop any one of us from moving there and buying a shovel?

So the good news is anybody who wants to be an artist can be. All it takes is (a) the desire and (b) the willingness to keep digging.

The important point is you are tapping into something else. You are being a channel.

Henry Miller, the famous writer and painter, tells us that any artist who really understands himself would be very humble.

"He would recognize himself as a man who has a certain faculty which he was destined to use for the service of others. He has nothing to be proud of, his name means nothing, he's only an instrument in a long procession."

Ideas and inventions and messages are floating around in the universe, seeking life, needing places to land. Our job is to be the air traffic controllers who steer them in.

Faulkner once said that if he hadn't written *The Sound and the Fury, Absalom, Absalom!, Requiem for a Nun,* and other books we now regard as classics, someone else would have written them.

The reason we idolize and canonize our artists is because they're transcribing important stuff. But they, the artist, are not the geniuses. The genius is the incredible stuff floating in the ether.

"The idea that I created this piece of music is kind of pompous," says Keith Richards of the Rolling Stones. "Music is everywhere: all you've got to do is pick it up. It's like being a receiver."

We're channels, people. Nothing more.

Remember Ouija boards we played with as kids? Back when we wanted to know who we were going to marry or whether or not Billy McDaniels even knew we were alive?

Put your fingertips gently on the plastic divining rod. Say a prayer. And begin.

Just do it!

DEVISE A SHOW IDEA
FOR *THE JERRY SPRINGER SHOW*

*"It could be that all awful dictators are frustrated
artists—Mao with his poetry and Mussolini with his
monuments. Stalin was once a journalistic hack.
Pol Pot left a very edgy photo collection behind.
And Osama seems quite interested in video."*

— P. J. O'ROURKE, HUMORIST

Create a character who could appear on *The Jerry Springer
Show* and send a letter from "him" or "her" requesting an
"audition." If you do get on, you've just landed your first acting gig.

Zumba for the Soul

- ⚭ Wear your pajamas to the movie theater.

- ⚭ Learn a card trick.

- ⚭ Sign up for Spanish (or French or German) lessons.

You're in Good Company

Norman Mailer, winner of two Pulitzer Prizes, didn't have the nerve to try out for his high school literary magazine, and a teacher at Harvard called his writing "fair."

WEEK 29

MYTH #7:
DOING ART REQUIRES
UNENDING SACRIFICE

*"The salvation you have been seeking elsewhere
has already arrived, woven into the very
warp and woof of your innermost self."*

— BOB SAVINO, KANSAS CITY SAGE AND POET

This week, we'll endeavor to overcome the misconception that doing art is hard work. That it involves perspiration, angst, and unceasing self-sacrifice.

Doing art is as natural as falling asleep, as easy as brushing your teeth.

Yes, it takes commitment. Yes, it takes time. But what, pray tell, is wrong with that? Would you really rather be sweeping the driveway, shopping for things you don't need?

Novelist John Irving claims it doesn't even take discipline.

"That's only needed for activities you don't enjoy. Sitting here and slipping into the lives of my characters is fun, it keeps me young," he says.

"But I'm not creative," you still insist on wailing.

Somewhere along the line we picked up the erroneous notion that doing art was excruciating except for the few lucky souls who are naturally "good at it."

Where did we get this erroneous notion? Certainly not from children. To a six-year-old, picking up a paintbrush, dipping it in a pot of paint, and rubbing it on a piece of paper is as natural as skipping or humming "Mary Had a Little Lamb." It's definitely a lot more natural than sitting still at dinner or tying a shoe.

What's hard is wasting time doing meaningless things, following cheap trinkets that may look good on the outside, but are as hollow as a piñata on the inside. In the arms of your imagination, you can dance unfettered on the moon.

"If you grew up in an African culture, you'd never think to question whether or not you were an artist," says David Darling, a former cellist with Paul Winter Consort. "It's a simple extension of what we are as human beings."

That's why Darling, who has more than three dozen highly acclaimed recordings and an international concert schedule, started Music for People workshops, which teach everyone to be a musician.

Teach is probably the wrong word because, as Darling says, "The concept that only certain people who play the right notes are musicians is unthinkable to someone in a tribal African culture. Music is simply joyful soundmaking, a celebration of movement and dance. It's part of a ritual honoring life."

Like so many things, we've cut off this part of ourselves that loves to sing. We were told by well-meaning teachers that our middle "C" was off tune and that our exuberance meter didn't mesh with the quartet.

At this point in your adult life, you'd probably rather French kiss a copperhead than sing in public. The shower—well, maybe—but as far as you're concerned, musical ability is like the fabled tortoise: it left you in the dust years ago.

Darling asks his students to hit themselves on the forehead every time they notice a negative thought coming up, such as:

I'm flubbing up.

I can't sing.

Sister Mary Margaret told me back in fourth grade I couldn't carry a tune in a bucket.

Before you know it, you look around the room and notice everyone is hitting themselves on the forehead—even the professionals who also come to Darling's workshops. He has worked with everyone from Bobby ("Don't Worry, Be Happy") McFerrin to Spyro Gyra to Peter, Paul and Mary.

"Feeling unworthy is so prevalent in the world that it's really amazing that human beings can feel good about anything," Darling said.

In his wildly provocative workshops, Darling offers a wide collection of unusual instruments, things you probably wouldn't find in your typical symphony orchestra. Darling's eclectic collection includes everything from accordions, banjos, and Japanese temple bells to kazoos, saws, and zithers.

After all, it's pretty hard to be too pretentious about music when you're playing a Mayan rain stick whose soft, lyrical rattle comes from the termite droppings inside.

This is why we need to approach art in a less pretentious way. Let's get out the kazoos, the finger paints, and the pots and pans that we used to bang on as kids.

"We've lost the sense of playing," Darling says. "We've disconnected from those dimensions of ourselves that our imaginations find so naturally. Adults, instead of encouraging us to play, tell us to 'go practice.'"

From the time you were a kid, you were taught to check your imagination at the door. Your imaginary friend, the one who whispered secrets in your ear, the one knows all about skipping and jumping rope, wasn't invited to school, to church, to the important "events" in life.

Invite her back. Send out a proper invitation. Draw it on the back of your grocery bag.

Just do it!

SPIT A BAR (AKA: WRITE A RAP SONG)

"When I graduated from high school, my teacher said I was throwing my life away following music. The same teacher later invited me back to speak at the school."

— BIG SEAN, AMERICAN RAPPER

You're going to lay down a rap this week. It needs a hook (kind of like the thesis of a term paper), a catchy beat, and lyrics. Try making something up on the spot. Or brainstorm some ideas. Either way, it'll be off the chain.

Now go perform it on a street corner.

Zumba for the Soul

- Create a new character for *Saturday Night Live*.

- Frame some leaves.

- Make a Valentine's card for the "one that got away."

You're in Good Company

Popular actress Lucille Ball, who earned a Lifetime Achievement Award from the Kennedy Center, was told repeatedly by her drama instructors that she'd never make it.

MYTH #8: ARTISTS ARE WEIRDOS, NOTHING LIKE YOU AND ME

"Art is the only way to run away without leaving home."

— TWYLA THARP, AMERICAN CHOREOGRAPHER

If you grow up in small-town Kansas like I did, you don't meet many filmmakers. Or actors. In fact, the only "artists" I ever saw (forget meeting) were the Ink Spots, a group of semi-professional has-beens who came to Ellsworth, Kansas (population 2,500), to sing their one hit, "If I Didn't Care," and dedicate the new gymnasium.

Because the average person doesn't interact with artists, we don't think of art as something possible for us. It never occurs to us to paint or make a film or write a play. We think of ourselves as "normal" people—people who teach school or drive busses or wait tables.

Artists are different. Mysterious, dark, brooding geniuses—definitely not somebody like you or your Uncle Seymour.

The media does nothing to dispel this air of mystery. They show us glamorous digs where famous writers and actresses take their vacations and tell us stories about the stars' oddball iguana collection or their 218th body piercing.

We forget they're human beings who probably eat Honey Nut Cheerios for breakfast just like we do.

We forget that making a film or writing a book is a process, a process that any of us can master if we want to.

The only difference between Woody Allen and you and me is that he believes he can make a film. You and I believe we can *see* a film. It never occurs to us to make one. We wouldn't know how.

But get this. You didn't know how to ride a bike either . . . until you learned.

Making anything—from a chocolate mousse to a bird-house to a five-part miniseries—has a recipe. Anyone who follows the recipe, learns the process, can produce the art.

Don't look at the projects in this book and think, *Oh, I could never write a country and western song*, or, *I don't know the first thing about dancing*. Remember what God said to Howard Finster, the Baptist preacher turned painter, when Finster told him he didn't know how to paint:

"How do you know?"

How do any of us know unless we try?

Woody Allen recalls the exact moment he first believed he could make a film. He was eight years old, watching Tyrone Power in *The Black Swan*, a swashbuckling pirate movie. He remembers thinking to himself, "Hey, I could do this." It was not a revelation that sent him out to find a movie camera, but it planted a seed—a seed that called to him, "You are capable of telling a story in this way."

Another time, when walking home from a movie, he found a strip of a half-dozen frames of 35-millimeter film near the theater's trash cans. It had broken off from the feature *Four Jills in a Jeep* with Phil Silvers and Carmen Miranda. He was mesmerized by the sight of the characters as he held the celluloid strip up to the sun.

In seeing that snippet of celluloid, he came to realize that movies aren't just magical fantasies to see on a Saturday afternoon (of course, he was also famous for seeing them on Tuesday, Wednesday, and Thursday afternoons, when he was supposed to be in school). They were created by human beings and there was a process for making one.

A process that he, Allan Stewart Konigsberg, small-potatoes boy from Brooklyn, could probably master. So what if his Jewish family was struggling, so what if he hated high school, dropped out of Brooklyn College. He, Allan Konigsberg (he didn't take his stage name until 1952), believed he could do it.

It's a startling revelation. That we could be filmmakers or painters. But it's the place all of us must start.

As long as we see art as something above us and artists as different than us, we will never be able to create our art.

Yeah, artists are prophets and visionaries and great talents, but so are you.

Just do it!

WRITE A FINAL CHAPTER

"You have to practice tuning out the noise of the culture to hear messages transmitted from your heart. Like a bird-watcher, an artist develops skills to spot and name quick flashes of awareness. When no one else sees the scarlet tanager, you can say with confidence, 'I saw it.'"

— ANI DIFRANCO, SINGER-SONGWRITER

You have 30 minutes to live. Write a story about what you'd do with these last precious moments.

It won't be graded. I won't send it to the Pulitzer Prize committee. You don't even have to show your mother if you don't want to. But write something. What would you eat? Drink? Who would you spend time with?

Zumba for the Soul

- ✺ Give to charity all the clothes you haven't worn in a year.

- ✺ Do the hokey pokey in the produce aisle at the grocery store.

- ✺ Stand up right now and proclaim, "I am a masterpiece. There is no one like me."

You're in Good Company

Georgia O'Keeffe was a commercial artist for years before she gained the strength to paint what she really wanted.

MYTH #9: CERTAIN CONDITIONS MUST BE IN PLACE TO CREATE ART

"An artist is someone who uses bravery, insight, creativity, and boldness to challenge the status quo."

— SETH GODIN, AUTHOR OF *PURPLE COW*

Bill Murray, taking a cab in the Bay Area, struck up a conversation with his driver.

"So," he asked. "What do you do when you're not driving bozos like me around?"

"I'm a sax player," his driver said.

"Do you practice?" Bill asked.

"Wish I could. I drive this cab 14 hours a day."

"So where's the sax now?"

"In the trunk."

"Well, pull over," Murray instructed. "I'll drive and you can practice."

As Murray explained to his audience at the rib joint where they also stopped on their monumental trip to Sausalito, "His sax playing made for a beautiful night."

It also punches a hole in the myth that certain conditions have to be in place for art to happen. This week, we're going to shred the last of the old templates. Don't even try to pull any of these excuses.

"I don't live in New York or Hollywood." Jeff Daniels lives in Chelsea, Michigan, a town of about 5,000. Jeff Bridges lives on a ranch in Montana. Sean Penn, after the 2010 earthquake, lived in a tent in Haiti.

When Crystal Bridges mounted their huge *State of the Art* exhibition, they found artists creating everywhere, from goat barns in the rural South to old pie factories in New England.

And need I remind you that Nelson Mandela wrote his memoir on hidden scraps of paper while in prison on Robben Island.

Where you are? Matters not one whit.

"I don't have the proper tools or the right equipment." Artist Jimmy Lee Sudduth started his prodigious career drawing with his fingers in the dirt outside his parents' front porch. Working in Fayette, Alabama, he found all his own "canvases"—plywood, doors, boards from demolished buildings—and made all his own "paint" using mud and pigments from such things as berries, motor oil, and plant juices.

Or consider fellow Alabama artist Thornton Dial, who incorporates everything from mangled Mickey Mouse dolls and mattress coils to strips of discarded American flags in his installations. Both these artists have been featured at the Smithsonian and MoMA. Neither had proper tools.

"Take stock in what you already have," says filmmaker Robert Rodriguez. "If your father owns a liquor store, make a movie about a liquor store. You've got a dog? Make a movie about your dog."

Art can be created from anything.

"I haven't mastered the right techniques to make a film, write a book, sell a song." Repeat after me: *there's no one way to create art.*

Again, to quote gonzo filmmaker Robert Rodriguez, "You don't need a fancy camera. You don't need a bunch of gear. You don't need a screenplay. You don't need great actors, a beautiful location, editing, or even money. The only thing you need is something to record a bunch of successive images on and a way to exhibit it."

"My stuff doesn't look like his/hers." Congratulations! You just created something original. You've got to learn to stand by your own work even if it's terrible. Especially when it's terrible.

"I can't get an art gallery or a literary agent to represent me." So what? Thanks to sites like Etsy, Zazzle, Yokaboo, and even Amazon Handmade, there are a gazillion ways to sell your art.

Countless artists are making a living (yet another myth—it can't be done) by managing their own websites, handling

their own sales, and developing a following independent of the old gallery model.

"I'm not naturally gifted like real artists." That's where practice comes in. Betty Edwards, author of *Drawing on the Right Side of the Brain*, compared creating art to reading. We don't give kids a stack of books and expect them to know how to read. We wouldn't accuse them of not having the aptitude for reading if they didn't pick it up on their own.

We all learned to read. We can all learn to produce art. It's a simple matter of learning the process and mustering the confidence to give it a whirl.

What treasure do you have, not to sell or to use to overcome anything, but simply to offer? What treasure have you been holding secret until now?

Just do it!

SCRIBBLE A POEM ON A PARK SIDEWALK

*"I wish artists would just wear a
T-shirt that says I'm a poet."*

— LIZ LAMOREUX, ARTIST

Yes, it would be nice if you wrote a poem of your own making, but if not, find a poem that speaks to your soul and introduce it to the park-going public. A telephone repairman in Kansas City uses different colored chalk to write his poems at Loose Park. He goes late at night when no one is there and leaves beautiful sentiments for people who come the next day.

And if you need a poem, feel free to use this one by my friend Virginia Petzold, who generously shared it in a Creating Miracles workshop I gave in New York last summer:

"What Matters Most"

Now I see past the illusion of my imaginary fear
For I believed a lie when I was
young . . . in such a tender year

The lie weighed hot and heavy like a stone
and so did cloud my inner grace
Because it made a home inside
my heart, an oh-so-tender space
A stone that was not really mine
to own, yet cast in my direction
And so I borrowed it for quite
some time . . . I gave it my attention
The stone was cold and rough and
made me feel not good enough
A stone that was not made of love,
that much is crystal clear
But rather made of judgment,
insecurity, and fear

As time went on it dimmed my
light and wrapped around my soul
Causing my dysfunction . . .
disconnection from the whole
Whole of all that's right and true for me
I traded truth and light for
who I thought that I must be
And so I fed the falseness of my fear
Of who I thought I was in such a tender year

Then somehow some creative
force inside me caused me to awaken
And feel the inner essence of
my soul that I'd so long forsaken
It was as if I'd heard the music
of some distant drum
I felt my true vibration . . .
my own magic hum

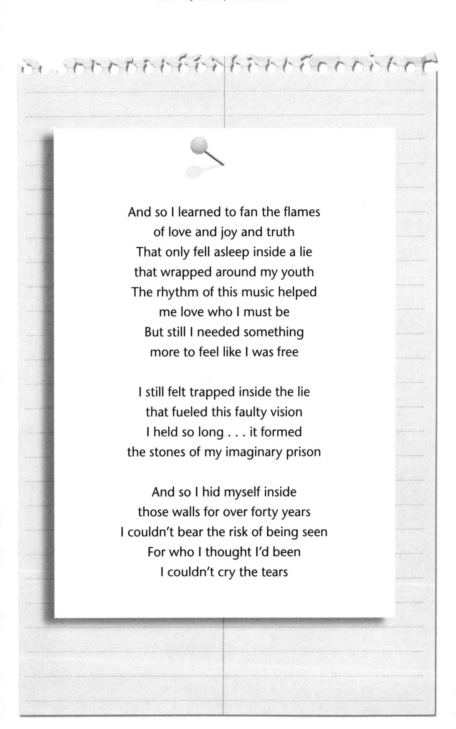

And so I learned to fan the flames
of love and joy and truth
That only fell asleep inside a lie
that wrapped around my youth
The rhythm of this music helped
me love who I must be
But still I needed something
more to feel like I was free

I still felt trapped inside the lie
that fueled this faulty vision
I held so long . . . it formed
the stones of my imaginary prison

And so I hid myself inside
those walls for over forty years
I couldn't bear the risk of being seen
For who I thought I'd been
I couldn't cry the tears

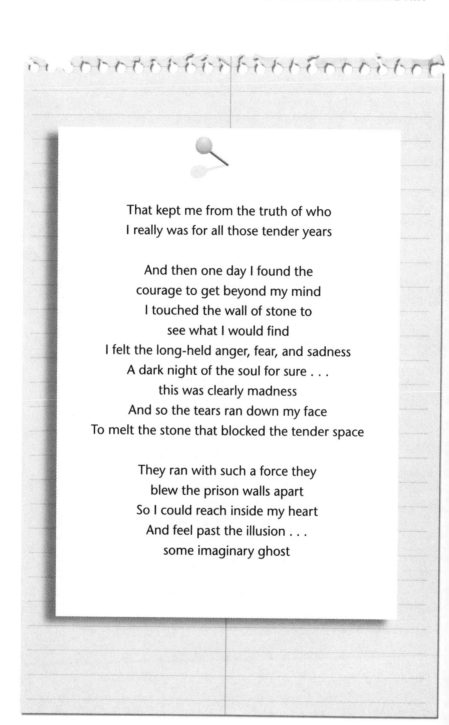

That kept me from the truth of who
I really was for all those tender years

And then one day I found the
courage to get beyond my mind
I touched the wall of stone to
see what I would find
I felt the long-held anger, fear, and sadness
A dark night of the soul for sure . . .
this was clearly madness
And so the tears ran down my face
To melt the stone that blocked the tender space

They ran with such a force they
blew the prison walls apart
So I could reach inside my heart
And feel past the illusion . . .
some imaginary ghost

Zumba for the Soul

- ⚮ Put on your favorite album and dance for 15 minutes.

- ⚮ Buy a lottery ticket and compose a plan for how you'd spend it.

- ⚮ Stage a story time.

You're in Good Company

Actress Carey Mulligan was rejected from every single drama school to which she applied. An auditor at Drama Centre London told the Academy Award nominee for best actress she could be a children's TV show presenter instead.

GENERATING CREATIVE CAPITAL

OR, WHY YOU SHOULD TELL NETFLIX WHERE TO GO

"Joy is in everything and anything we might experience. We just have to have the courage to turn against our habitual lifestyle and engage in unconventional living."

— JON KRAKAUER,
AMERICAN WRITER AND MOUNTAINEER

Monetary limitations often serve as handy excuses for why we refuse to say, "Who's there?" when the muse calls out, "Knock-knock."

It usually goes something like this:

> *I will follow my dream, I'm sure I will, just as soon as I save up the money, just as soon as I don't need to pay rent.*

I'd like to throw some shade on this extremely shoddy defense.

I can't disregard the fact we have commercialized nearly every single thing we used to do for passion. And, yes, the notion that financial capital is hard to come by holds a lot of sway.

But here's the thing. Money and creativity have absolutely nothing in common.

Creative capital, unlike financial capital, is virtually unlimited. It has no floor, no ceiling. And every last one of us has total access.

The muses have a limitless supply of songs, films, books, inventions, and lots of other brilliant things that I can't name because they haven't been made manifest just yet. At all times, the muses are advertising for folks like us to pilot their projects into existence.

To access your God-given creative capital, simply begin moving toward the thing that makes you feel most alive. The thing you'd do if you'd never heard the word *money*. You'll recognize it when you feel goose bumps, when you notice the excitement and joy in your body.

"But, but . . . who will pay me when I'm writing my book, composing my theme song?"

And to that I have one answer. Who pays you to binge-watch Netflix? Who sends a paycheck for those hours you spend trawling Facebook?

All of us have the ability to build empires out of our imagination. In this section, we'll look at examples of real-life creators who spun gold out of their crazy schemes.

Generating creative capital is holy work. All of us are called.

WEEK 32

POWER OF THE PURPLE CRAYON

"Like a loyal animal, the imagination will come when it knows the door is open."

— CAROL LLOYD, FOUNDER OF
SAN FRANCISCO'S THE WRITING PARLOR

My favorite how-to book will never be found in the self-help section of your local bookstore. It was written long before the term *self-help* was even coined.

It's a children's book called *Harold and the Purple Crayon*, and it says more about the possibilities of the human condition than anything positive-thinking Norman Vincent Peale could ever cook up.

Written by Crockett Johnson in 1955, this 65-page masterpiece tells the story of a little boy named Harold who decides to go out for a walk one evening. When there isn't any moonlight (and, of course, everyone knows a good walk requires moonlight), Harold takes out his purple crayon and draws the moon.

He also needs a sidewalk (which he draws) that leads to a forest (he only draws one tree because he doesn't want to get lost) that turns out to be an apple tree (or at least it is after Harold's crayon gets hold of it). Unfortunately, the apples aren't ripe yet, so Harold draws a frightening dragon to guard the tree.

When he falls into the ocean, Harold is able to gather his wits and his purple crayon to draw a boat and set sail for a beach, where he draws a picnic lunch with nine kinds of pie.

The whole book is about Harold's great adventures scaling a mountain, soaring in a hot air balloon, and touring a city, all created by his ever-faithful purple crayon.

It's a powerful book because it demonstrates a great spiritual truth—we are the authors of our own lives. We draw every detail—even the dragons and the oceans we "accidentally" fall into.

Harold could have gone on his walk, noticed there was no moon, and sat down and pouted. Isn't that what most of us do? Damn, no moon. I'd better call my therapist, hit some pillows. He could have drawn his moon, compared it to El Greco, and said, "I am a hopeless sham. I'll never be an artist."

Instead, he kept reaching for his purple crayon and drawing every event, every answer, every friend that he needed. We all have that power. We can strike out for the Great Wall of China, lunch at the Savoy, fly a glider down the Pacific coast, and still be back at our desk for a 10 o'clock meeting.

Harold was a kid. He hadn't yet lost his imagination, his sense of wonder and awe. No one had explained yet that he couldn't have whatever he wanted. As long as he had his purple crayon, he could ride the universe.

In today's world, crayons and creativity might as well be the same thing. How many adults do you know who still have crayons?

Remember that big box of Crayola Crayons with 64 colors—everything from apricot to fuchsia to forest green? With that one small gold-and-green box, you could have anything your little heart desired—navy blue carousels with peach prancing ponies, magenta castles with yellow-green drawbridges, and purple grass, although your teacher might have frowned on that kind of thing. Grass is green, don't you know?

Each year of school, however, the Crayola stash gets smaller. By the time we graduate from high school, we're wielding nothing but a blue Bic pen.

Let's go out this week and get some crayons. Let's create the world to our liking. And if we happen to fall into an ocean or run into a dragon, we'll just draw ourselves a lifeboat and head for the beach where at least one kind of pie will be waiting.

Just do it!

PRODUCE A MEMOIR OF YOUR FIRST DATE

"Make your own things. Even if it's just a short play with friends or a movie you put on YouTube. It helps you figure out what you're good at. And it gives you community quickly. You get more from it than it takes from you."

— GRETA GERWIG, ACTRESS

Don't even try pretending you can't remember your first date. Few things inspire more striking emotions. What did you wear? Where did you go? What was your biggest fear? Did you ever go out with him or her again?

Zumba for the Soul

- ♪ Take a card table to the park and host a gin rummy tournament.

- ♪ Pull something out of your pantry and draw it.

- ♪ Eat something you've never tried.

You're in Good Company

Steve Winwood, honored by *Rolling Stone* as one of the 100 greatest singers of all time, was kicked out of the Birmingham and Midland Institute of Music.

YA GOTTA BELIEVE

*"If your heart is pulling you in a direction that
has mystery and wonder, trust it and follow it."*

— DAVID WILCOX, SONGWRITER

In January 1959, a 30-year-old 8th grade dropout from Detroit borrowed $800 from a family savings plan to buy a
house, not an unusual goal for a man of his age. Only this
enterprising 30-year-old had his sights set a little higher. He
was going to use that unassuming two-story house to start a
record company.

The man, of course, is Berry Gordy, the record company
is Motown, and the plan, well, let's just say that it worked.
Between 1959 and 1972, Gordy's Motown released 535
singles, 75 percent of which made the pop charts. From a
recording studio that's barely larger than a king-size bed,

Gordy produced 60 number-one hits before he moved to Hollywood and sold Motown to MCA Records for $61 million.

I tell you this story because it demonstrates the power of opening to a bigger possibility. Berry Gordy could have easily settled for less. He was black at a time when black wasn't yet considered universally beautiful. He dropped out of school, had already failed at an upstart boxing career, and could neither play an instrument nor read music.

But he had a dream. He wanted to write songs. And if nobody else would produce them, well, he'd just do it himself.

Catching a dream is the point at which all of us must start. We see a vision. We hear a tapping on our heart. We start to wonder if "maybe, just maybe, we might be able to" write a song, dance a poem, leap into a new way of being. We become willing to say "it *is* possible."

But not even Gordy could have known that when he recruited a 19-year-old Smokey Robinson and his high school quartet, the Matadors (later to become the Miracles), he was launching one of the biggest musical phenomenons of our times.

When we first begin to listen to our dreams, we don't always know where they're leading us. This is good news. If we could see the final outcome, we might get scared off, put on the brakes, think, *Whoa Nelly, that's way too big for me.* So, luckily, all we have to do for now is take that first step, put that first toe out the door.

The other thing the Motown phenomenon demonstrates is the wealth of talent that so often goes undiscovered. Had Berry Gordy been content to plug lug nuts at a Detroit auto plant, one of many jobs he tried before starting Motown, he would have never plucked Diana Ross, Stevie Wonder, and hundreds of other poor black kids out of the ghetto. It seems impossible that superstars of their stature might have taken another path. But had Diana Ross not caught a vision, she could very well be just another bag lady on 9th Street; Stevie Wonder, another blind kid on welfare. Thank God, they had the opportunity to tap the creative spirit within.

If Gordy hadn't turned 2648 West Grand Boulevard into a "happening" place to be, "I Heard It Through the Grapevine," "Ain't No Mountain High Enough," "I'll Be There," and thousands of other songs would never have been written.

I, for one, would have had a completely different upbringing. If it wasn't for the Four Tops' hit, "Reach Out I'll Be There," I'd have never danced with Andy Gilmore at Jim Rinklemeyer's party. I'd have never known he wore Brut cologne, never known he smelled like mothballs, a discovery that can undoubtedly be traced to the tweed jacket he'd stolen from his older brother's closet, and never known how it felt to be 13 and helplessly smitten. Unfortunately, I lacked the nerve to ever speak to him again.

How many of us lack the nerve to investigate the creative spirit within us? How many of us are on spiritual "welfare" because we haven't caught the vision? The same kind of talent Gordy found in his protégés is hidden in the people we walk by every day. It's hidden because nobody bothered to look, nobody bothered to say, "Hey, look what we can do." It's hidden behind thoughts of unworthiness, behind "masks" that we put on for a good show.

Each and every one of us has that same creative spirit. But, no, you're probably thinking Detroit was different. The list of superstars goes on and on—the Temps, the Tops, the Supremes. But you know what? Gordy could have just as easily opened that record company and been just as successful in Cleveland or Chicago or Omaha, Nebraska, for that matter. There are Temps, Tops, Supremes everywhere. People just as

talented, just as musical. The only thing they don't have is Gordy's vision.

This is not to deny the huge talent that existed in Detroit at that time. What they did on that little three-track recording system in Studio A can only be described as the musical equivalent of sitting in the front of the bus.

But it only happened because one man was willing to step up to the plate, was willing to say, "I believe."

Just do it!

PLAY CARPOOL KARAOKE

"The arts are so good to those who practice them."
— KURT VONNEGUT, AUTHOR

If you haven't seen James Corden's online sensation, Carpool Karaoke, where he and a recording megastar drive around LA belting out the star's greatest hits, you must not be on Facebook.

First, let me say congratulations, followed by, there's something really joyful about watching famous people sing their own songs in an ordinary situation without their 'teams' primping, directing, smoothing out all bumps.

Carpool Karaoke is ridiculously simple: it's just James, a fixed camera, and stars like Justin Bieber, Adele, Stevie Wonder, and even Michelle Obama riding shotgun. They're singing and chatting candidly as they deal with traffic jams, carpool lanes, and drive-through restaurants. In one episode, Jennifer Hudson sang Corden's Whopper order.

So this week, you're going to grab a friend, hook up your smartphone, and play your own carpool karaoke. Whether or not you put it on Facebook? Up to you.

Zumba for the Soul

- Create a new kind of pie.
- Come up with a new constitutional amendment.
- Design a tree house.

You're in Good Company

In 1954, Elvis Presley was fired by the Grand Ole Opry after one performance. Manager Jimmy Denny told Elvis, "You ain't going nowhere, son. You ought to go back to driving a truck."

FOLLOWING BREAD CRUMBS

"When a man undertakes to create something, he establishes a new heaven, a new firmament, a new source of energy."

— PHILIPPUS AUREOLUS PARACELSUS, SWISS PHYSICIAN, PHILOSOPHER, AND ASTROLOGER

At last count, the 2002 novel *The Secret Life of Bees* had sold 6 million copies, been translated into 35 languages, and was made into a movie starring Queen Latifah, Alicia Keys, and Dakota Fanning. But it would never have been written if its author, Sue Monk Kidd, hadn't been bold and reckless enough to ask for what she wanted and to follow the bread crumbs that led to her creative capital.

In 1993, at a convent in Palianis on the Greek island of Crete, Kidd bowed before a dark-faced icon of a Virgin Mary. She humbly asked for the courage to become a novelist. She always knew she wanted to write, even though her fear of making a decent living at it convinced her to get a nursing degree and work as an RN until she was 29. Until that day when she dared utter her dream out loud to the icon hanging from a gnarly tree branch, she mainly wrote inspirational nonfiction, documenting stories from her life with her husband Sandy and her two kids.

She returned from Greece and wrote a first chapter about a girl whose bedroom wall is full of bees. She took it to a writer's conference where the professor who was teaching it called it "interesting, but with small potential." Even though she was being nudged to write a book, she turned that chapter into a short story and promptly forgot about it. Except not really.

It percolated in her mind for six years. Six years and a couple of nonfiction books later, she was in Greece again, this time on a postgraduation trip with her daughter Ann. Only now she was approaching menopause and her unrequited dream of being a novelist was still banging around inside her heart, still trying to make its presence known. At Ephesus, in an olive grove outside the little home where Mary once lived, she decided to ask again.

As she wondered in her memoir, *Traveling with Pomegranates*, "When we send prayers into the universe, are they heard? Can they change anything? Or are our supplications a form of magical thinking?"

It had been a long while since she'd made a concrete petition, but she asked again about the novel. She wanted guidance, a clear sign.

No sooner did she leave the little prayer chapel to rejoin her daughter than a bee landed on her left shoulder. Ann reached reflexively to wave it away, but Sue put out her hand, shaking her head, as if to say, "No. It's a bee. A *bee*."

They walked down the hill, beside the spring with holy water. The bee held its ground, rode back to the tour bus on Sue's shoulder.

"What's with this bee?" Ann asked, genuinely affected. "It's like it has adopted you."

"It's telling me I'm about to go home and finish up that novel I started six years ago," Sue said.

Just do it!

NAME YOUR DEBUT CD

"Even God can't steer a parked car."

— MARY OMWAKE, UNITY MINISTER

Hey, I didn't say you had to write the songs. All you have to do is come up with a clever (maybe you prefer meaningful?) name for the debut that will undoubtedly feature you skipping down a beach or maybe playing air guitar.

Zumba for the Soul

- Invent a new kind of pizza.
- Buy a CD that hasn't made the pop charts.
- Have a picnic at the park for breakfast.

You're in Good Company

New Yorker columnist Calvin Trillin calls his predraft a "vomit out" where he writes anything at all that comes to mind. He often worries that someone might see it before he gets around to cleaning it up.

OH, THE THINKS YOU CAN THINK

"The role of the artist is not to find solutions, but to compel us to love life in all its countless, inexhaustible manifestations."

— LEO TOLSTOY, WRITER

Dr. Seuss wrote 47 books, won 3 Academy Awards, and landed the prestigious Pulitzer Prize.

But until the day of his death at age 87, he maintained that his incredible success was "mostly luck." His first children's book, *And to Think That I Saw It on Mulberry Street*, was rejected by 27 publishers. They thought it was "too different" and "didn't have a moral or a message."

At 32, Ted Geisel (Dr. Seuss was a pen name he manufactured in college) decided his quest to publish a book was futile. He marched out of the office of that 27th publisher with a firm conviction that the only sensible thing to do was stage a ceremonial burning of the manuscript he'd worked on for so long. So much for creative capital.

As he strode grimly down Madison Avenue, his head down, he was hailed by an old friend from college.

"Hey, what's that under your arm?" asked Mike McClintock, the friend who was a year behind him at Dartmouth.

Dejectedly, Geisel told him it was "nothing, just a book he was going home to burn."

McClintock, who had three hours earlier been appointed juvenile editor of Vanguard Press, said, "Hey, we're standing outside my office. Let's go up and look at it."

"If I had been going down the other side of Madison Avenue, I'd be in the dry cleaning business today," said Geisel.

Was it luck? I prefer to think of Geisel's chance meeting with an old college buddy as a near-perfect example of Louis Pasteur's famous credo, "fortune favors the prepared mind."

Geisel spent his life generating creative capital. He'd been drawing since he was a kid, penciling cows with angel wings and dogs crossing tight wires in the margins of his school notebooks.

Geisel called it luck. I call it enticing evidence that when you make the commitment to be there for your art, a whole choir of angels and a 20-piece orchestra will sign on to accompany you.

Geisel once said the best piece of advice he could dispense was "write a verse a day, not to send to publishers, but to throw in wastebaskets."

He also counseled young artists to "paint at least one picture a month just for fun."

In other words, practice, practice, practice.

It doesn't require hours, but do a little something every single day. Write a haiku (how hard can 17 syllables be?) or make up a jingle for a product you use. Or draw a new hat for the Cat in the Hat.

Just do it!

DRAW ONE OR MORE OF THE FOLLOWING

*"Hope and creativity are two of the
most important things in the world."*

— EMMA STONE, ACTRESS

Take your pick. Or better yet, draw all 11.

1. Three Stooges. (Nyuk-nyuk-nyuk.)

2. A giraffe. (Stick your neck out.)

3. A coffee cup.

4. An alien.

5. Batman.

6. A mouth.

7. A panda.

8. An owl.

9. Your bedroom.

10. Your first pet.

11. The cat's new hat!

Got a pencil? Ready, set, go.

Zumba for the Soul

- Stage a charades party.
- Celebrate the full moon.
- Draw your fairy godmother.

You're in Good Company

Rudyard Kipling, author of *The Jungle Book*, was fired as contributor to the *San Francisco Examiner* in 1889. His editor said, "I'm sorry, Mr. Kipling, but you just don't have the proper command of the English language."

WEEK 36

PET ROCKS, NUTS, AND DUCT TAPE

*"Everything you are and do and say is filled with God:
the trees, the asphalt, the people fighting over Aqua
Net at Walmart. That sounds silly, but silliness is just as
important as love, just as important as tragedy."*

— DONALD ROLLER WILSON, ARTIST

When I was 23, a fortune teller from Jamaica took one look at my left palm and pronounced that my biggest problem would be deciding which of my many interests to pursue. At the time, I was designing clothes (things like too-tight yellow jumpsuits with jacks and rubber balls on the zipper pull tabs), playing rugby, writing articles, and trying to break into the world of incentive travel hosting.

Still, today, I dabble in many genres. I've written a children's book, a screenplay, several novels, and hundreds of magazine articles on everything from bungee jumping in New Zealand to carpet buying in Morocco. In other words, it's hard to pin me down.

If you're having trouble pinning down the artistic genre you most want to pursue, maybe it's because your genre hasn't been invented yet. Perhaps you should invent your own.

Whole careers have been made from such innovation. Los Angeles artist Kim Abeles uses smog to make art. She cuts out detailed stencils and lays them outside on Plexiglas where they collect microscopic bits of car exhaust and factory emissions. From smog, she has stenciled everything from murky brown tables complete with dinner for two to a series of presidential plates. Woodrow Wilson, who encouraged responsible industry in his inaugural address, only stayed out in the smog for four days. George Bush, on the other hand, got 40 days.

Chris Wink, cofounder of the Blue Man Group, said that although he was attracted to the arts, he didn't have the skills to be a fine artist. "People talk about following your bliss, which is wonderful if your bliss happens to fit into a neat category like, 'I want to be an evolutionary biologist.' I couldn't follow my bliss, because I had blisses."

As a performance artist, he paints himself blue, drums, comments on contemporary culture, and catches marshmallows in his mouth.

"At a certain point, I made my brain a secondary organ and listened to my gut: 'Find a way to combine all your blisses and, who the f*ck cares if you're a waiter.' I had to rid myself of my immaturity and insecurities. I had to develop my own self," he says.

Writer Ted L. Nancy created a whole new genre of writing by sending ridiculously loony letters to various companies.

With the support of Jerry Seinfeld who first sent the letters to his agent, Nancy's letters were collected in the book *Letters from a Nut*, which proved to be a phenomenal success.

Nancy wrote to the Coca-Cola company inquiring whether his beverage, Kiet Doke, interferes with their beverage; to the San Diego Padres asking if he can attend a game with a portable shower on his head (because his medical condition requires his head to be kept in a vinyl enclosure); and to a Las Vegas casino wondering, as a 675-pound George Harrison look-alike, if they'd be interested in booking his band, the Fat Beatles! "Tubby Paul, weighing 490 pounds," he added, "is the cute Fat Beatle."

Seinfield asks in his introduction to the second *Nuts* book, "Instead of being sidetracked with these imbecilic missives, shouldn't people be doing their jobs and contributing to the growth of our nation?"

In other words, isn't all this silliness a waste of time?

I think not. In fact, I'd venture to say we need *more* silliness, more willingness to look like a crackpot.

The word *silly* was originally the middle English word *sillig*, which meant "blessing."

If all us would be willing to do three silly things a day, things like attaching toilet paper rolls to our feet or howling on traffic-jammed freeways (things humor consultant C. W. Metcalf did to overcome his case of terminal seriousness), we would unquestionably receive more blessings.

We would be freer to break new paths, to find new adventures. As creators, we are not here to do what has already been done.

Maybe all of us should loosen up a bit and hitch our dreams to a sillier star.

As an old children's song says, "Boom, boom, ain't it great to be crazy."

Just do it!

WRITE THE TITLES FOR FIVE COUNTRY AND WESTERN SONGS

"Part of the process of writing is not so much to explain your vision, but to discover it."

— ROBERT TOWNE, SCREENWRITER

It doesn't matter if you've never written a song. You have permission to write a really awful country and western song. Or maybe a good one. Sometimes, when we give ourselves permission to be less than perfect, brilliance surfaces.

Your job is to come up with either one song or five country and western song titles. Remember, they're often funny and often involve heartbreak, mamas, and trucks.

I once wrote a C&W song at Sony Studios in Nashville with a famous songwriter. We titled our masterpiece: "Our Baby's Ugly and It's Not My Fault."

Zumba for the Soul

- ✺ Dress like your favorite movie character.
- ✺ Audit a class.
- ✺ Write a thank you letter to God—mail it.

You're in Good Company

Kurt Vonnegut, author of 14 American classics, once said, "When I write, I feel like an armless, legless man with a crayon in his mouth."

CREATIVE ACCOMPLICES

"I am my own experiment. I am my own work of art."

— MADONNA, SINGER-SONGWRITER

When Sting was given an old, out-of-tune guitar with rusty strings, he felt as if he'd been given a friend for life, an accomplice to help him get out of Wallsend, England, where he grew up.

He was eight at the time and he'd already decided he didn't want to build ships like the thousands of men who walked by his house on their way to the shipyard every morning. It was a hard life, he noticed—noisy and dangerous with toxic work conditions.

Although his dad was a milkman, his grandfather had been a shipwright and, as a child, Sting anxiously wondered if that was to be his destiny. There weren't many other jobs in his hometown on the northeast coast of England.

"But once I was bequeathed that battered old guitar, I quickly realized I'd found a coconspirator to help me escape from this industrial landscape," he said.

"My dream was to leave this town just like those ships that never came back once they were launched. I wanted to be a writer of songs, to sing those songs to vast numbers of people all over the world and to be paid extravagant amounts of money."

The dream started one day when the Queen Mother came to his town to break a bottle of champagne on the bow of one of the ships. His mother forced him and his brother and sisters to dress up in their Sunday finest as the motor-cade passed in front of their tiny home in the shadow of the shipyard.

"It wasn't that long ago that the Royal Family were thought to have magical powers. People held up their sick children, hoping to touch the hem of the king, hoping for a cure," Sting said. "It wasn't like that in my day, but it was still really exciting when Princess Anne or one of the royals came to give a speech.

"I was standing there waving my little Union Jack and there in a big, black Rolls Royce was the Queen Mother. She seemed to acknowledge me. She looked me in the eye. I smiled. She smiled. We had a moment.

"I wasn't cured of anything. It was the opposite actually. I was infected with an idea. I realized I didn't belong in the street. I didn't want to work in the shipyard. I wanted to be in that car. I wanted a bigger life. A life out of the ordinary."

And that's how it begins. When we take the time to listen.

Just do it!

PIONEER FIVE USES FOR A CARDBOARD BOX

"To invent, you need a good imagination and a pile of junk."

— THOMAS A. EDISON, AMERICAN INVENTOR

Ninety percent of all products shipped in the United States still come in good old cardboard boxes. Luckily, the ubiquitous box can be broken down and recycled, but this week, instead of tossing them into the bin, you're going to invent five alternative uses. Again, you don't have to actually make them, just use your magic wand of imagination. I've seen repurposed boxes made into weaving looms, mazes, a Rapunzel castle, and a shadow theater.

Zumba for the Soul

- Buy tomato plants for all your friends and deliver them with three recipes.

- Learn all the native flowers of your state. Find at least five of them.

- Make a paper airplane out of brightly colored paper.

You're in Good Company

Even the great Don Henley, after releasing a whopping 25 Top 40 hits, is not immune to self-doubt. He says, "Who am I to be doing this? Why do I deserve to get my feelings and opinions on this blank piece of vinyl that a million people are going to hear? Always, I must overcome those feelings of in-adequacy, those feelings of 'I don't deserve this.'"

WEEK 38

THE PEARL OF FAILURE

"I always said I wanted to be somebody.
I guess I should have been more specific."

— LILY TOMLIN, ACTRESS AND COMEDIAN

World War I was over and Walt Disney, who joined the Red Cross Ambulance Service by forging his parent's signature, had a dream. So what if he was only 18, a kid compared to the rest of the staff at the *Kansas City Star*.

His burning ambition, the dream that kept him going through long, tedious days chauffeuring boisterous colonels around France and delivering beans and sugar to military hospitals, was the thought of a cartoonist job at his home-town newspaper, the *Star*.

He'd already thrown newspapers for the venerable publishing company, getting up every morning at 3:30 to neatly roll and prepare the morning news for eager readers. Each dawn, as he leafed through the paper, admiring the drawings of the cartoonists who graced the editorial pages, he'd think, *Someday, that will be me.*

Now that he was back from the war, surely the *Star* would be thrilled to hire such an up-and-coming artist.

He gathered his portfolio, barged into the office of the newspaper's employment director, and waited, pen poised, to sign his W-4. But instead of the "welcome aboard" he expected, the kindly gentleman said, "Sorry, can't use you."

Talk about defeat. Disney's highest aspiration had just been ground into little pieces.

How was he to know that life had something bigger in store?

If he'd have been like most of us, he would have retreated, tail between his legs, into the basement. He'd have listened to that voice that haunts all of us, the voice that says, "See, I told you you were no good."

He could have listened to that voice again when a few months later, Pressman-Rubin Studios, an ad agency that hired him to draw farm equipment, laid him off after one short month because of his "singular lack of drawing ability."

Sure, it took him a while to lick his wounds, but by the time he was 21, he was using that same "lack of drawing ability" to create Laugh-O-Grams, animated reels of Kansas City residents interspersed with news headlines, public service announcements, and jokes told by Disney's first animated character, Professor Whosis. They were popular enough that Disney was able to hire animators (he offered "free animation lessons" to anyone interested in the cartoon business) to join him in the family garage.

Disney's dream grew bigger. He wanted to reach an audience larger than Kansas City, to create a cartoon that would appeal to a national distributor. Writing a simple adaptation of "Little Red Riding Hood" and shooting it entirely with his single hand-cranked camera, he talked the general manager of the chain of theaters that showed Laugh-O-Grams into sending prints to New York distributors. Every major distributor said, "No." The one small company that liked it enough to send a $100 advance proceeded to go belly-up within a month.

By 1923, even though he'd received $500 for a short called *Tommy Tucker's Tooth*, produced for a local dentist, Disney's five newly hired animators had quit and Laugh-O-Grams had collapsed into insolvency.

Another defeat. Another failure.

So next time your dreams hit a dead end, think of Walt Disney. Realize that maybe the reason your dreams aren't coming true is because they're not quite big enough yet.

Maybe your vision is ahead of its time and the playing field you're suiting up for isn't big enough to hold you.

Disney thought making it as a *Kansas City Star* cartoonist would give him everything he needed.

Had he met his "highest" dream, the *Star* would have had a so-so editorial cartoonist, a guy none of us would have ever heard of. There would be no Mickey Mouse, no Disneyland. My friend Kitty would never be able to do her Donald Duck imitation.

All I can say is thank goodness Walt Disney was a failure.

Just do it!

CREATE A COMIC BOOK CHARACTER

"Life is like a ten-speed bicycle.
Most of us have gears we never use."

— CHARLES M. SCHULZ, COMIC BOOK ARTIST

Poor Charlie Brown! His kite always gets stuck in a tree, his advice-giving friend Lucy has the gall to charge five cents per session, and his dog, Snoopy, keeps picking fights with the Red Baron.

Cathy Guisewite was an ad hack until she created *Cathy*, which spoke to a whole generation of single female baby boomers.

Your job this week is to create an imaginary character. Make him or her come to life. Know everything about his habits, her likes and dislikes, his tics and idiosyncrasies.

What does he like for breakfast? Has she ever been married? What did her parents do? What is her favorite song? Where does he work? Pick a name and just start writing.

Zumba for the Soul

❧ Design a garden.

❧ Make a paper doll of your first boyfriend or girlfriend.

❧ Have a 15-minute conversation with your body.

You're in Good Company

Richard Bach's 10,000-word story about a "soaring seagull" was rejected 18 times before Macmillan finally published it in 1970. By 1975, it had sold more than 7 million copies in the U.S. alone.

GETTING JIGGY WITH IT

"We're all stuck here together on this small planet."

— MATT HARDING, TRAVELER AND
INTERNET CELEBRITY

Matt Harding had what some might call a "lack of clear direction." Other than playing video games, he wasn't sure what he wanted to do with his 70 or so years on the planet. His dad, frustrated by his son's lack of ambition, finally severed his college funds, forcing Matt to go out and join the labor force. That's what responsible adults do, right? Sell their soul to "the *man*."

But Matt wasn't content to follow the responsible adult rules. He refused to settle for the customary 9–5. He wanted to travel, to see the world, to visit as many countries as he possibly could.

The voice that pushes us toward the soul-numbing amassment of legal tender laughed in his face.

"You can't do that without a big bank account, without a high-paying job with lots of vacation. Fahgetaboutit!"

But Matt didn't listen. He worked as long as it took to save up some money. Then he quit his job and hit the road once again. He traveled until "lack of moola" forced him back into a cubicle, ever expanding his vision of new countries to add to his "life list." One day, while hanging out in Hanoi, a fortuitous event caused his creative capital to flower. Matt's buddy, armed with a video camera, prodded him: "Hey, go do that weird dance you do. I'll tape it."

The weird dance, in case you haven't been lucky enough to see Matt's now-infamous YouTube video, is a kooky arm-flapping, knee-marching step that adolescent boys fancy at junior high dances. His buddy videotaped him performing it on the streets of Hanoi. And then in Tonga. And then the Philippines, Mali, and beside the Panama Canal. His sister, who was trying to keep up with her wayfaring brother, begged him to start a website with videos of him doing the crazy dance. Like a virus, "Where the Hell is Matt?"—the aptly named video of a grinning Matt bouncing in 69 countries—spread from computer to computer.

Before he knew it, his video had more than 12 million hits and Matt had become an overnight celebrity. He was interviewed by *The Washington Post*, Jimmy Kimmel, and *National Geographic*. Visa hired him to do a TV commercial. NASA put his dancing video on their Astronomy Picture of the Day website. And as for building creative capital, Stride Gum approached him about making a video for their website. They wanted Matt to dance and get others all over the world to dance with him. And, of course, they agreed to pick up the tab.

Just do it!

DESIGN A TAROT CARD

"To draw, you must close your eyes and sing."
— PABLO PICASSO, SPANISH ARTIST

Notice, I didn't suggest making a tarot *deck*. The project is to make one card. Cards are small—much easier than decorating, say, the side of a barn. It's a project of creation, not divination.

If you want, you can make your own version of one of your favorite cards—say the High Priestess, the Hermit, or the Five of Cups. Or you can come up with your own character. A troubadour? A mermaid?

Zumba for the Soul

- Hug 14 people.
- Rent your favorite Disney cartoon and eat gummy worms.
- Camp out in the backyard.

You're in Good Company

Maya Angelou, author of I Know Why the Caged Bird Sings and many other bestsellers, says, "Every time I write a book, every time I face that yellow pad, the challenge is so great. I have written eleven books, but each time I think, Oh, they're going to find out now. I've run a game on everybody and they're going to find me out."

254

YES AND . . .

"I can't think of any way to explain the existence of art other than as a means to express something greater than ourselves. I can't reach a single musical decision except with the goal of making a connection to God."

— SOFIA GUBAIDULINA, RUSSIAN COMPOSER

Tyler Perry was not always the successful producer, director, and actor he is today. Two scars on his wrist depict an earlier "plan" he had for his life. He was born in New Orleans, the oldest of four kids of a sometimes-employed carpenter and a mom who worked as a poorly paid preschool teacher. But living in poverty was not the worst of it. Perry's uneducated dad, orphaned at age two, hadn't developed the best parenting skills. Emmitt Perry had a tendency to beat his asthmatic son in a misguided attempt to toughen him up, to make him strong.

In his attempt to escape his unhappy childhood, Tyler spent a lot of time daydreaming. He created fictional worlds that were the exact opposite of his own life. He wrote and illustrated stories about kids who lived in mansions, kids who had pets, kids who were happy.

At 16, Tyler Perry dropped out of school and changed his name (he was born Emmitt Jr.) to escape any association with the dad he despised.

When he was 21, he was sitting at home one day when Oprah came on. The Queen of Talk suggested to her audience they should write down their feelings toward people who had hurt them. She said it was cathartic. After he looked up the word *cathartic* in the dictionary, Perry began pouring out his feelings toward his father, his mother, the life of poverty by which he felt victimized. Pages and pages streamed out of him, eventually prompting him to think, "Man, I ought to turn this into a play."

Most people would have called him crazy. He's a high school dropout, for goodness' sake. He doesn't know the first thing about writing plays.

But the creativity seed was planted, the inner decision was made. The ball began to roll. He started to discover what he now calls "God's little flashes of light."

His Oprah assignment turned into the creative capital of a play, a real play he called *I Know I've Been Changed*. Working odd jobs such as used car salesman and bill collector, he managed to scrimp together $12,000 to stage the play.

Unfortunately, it bombed. A grand total of 30 people showed up opening weekend, most of whom were friends. Many might have stopped there, but Perry's creative capital had begun to accumulate. He had caught fire. Too late to erect any more "not good enough, not smart enough" blocks. For six years, he tweaked the play, staging it again and again. Each time, it bombed, driving him further and further off a financial precipice. For six months, he even lived in his car, homeless, frustrated, and wondering why he ever thought it was a good idea to listen to Oprah.

Fast-forward to February 1998. He decided to give it one last chance. On opening night, the heater broke in the dressing room of the Atlanta church-turned-theater he had rented for his final attempt to follow his dream. As he sat there freezing, he told himself in no uncertain terms, "This is it. I'm going to follow my mom's advice. I'm going to give up this crazy dream. I must have been wrong."

But as he peeked out from behind the curtain, he saw lines of people waiting to get in. That play sold out its three-night run. And his next play, a collaboration with a Dallas minister, raked in $5 million in five months. Today, as one of the highest-paid men in Hollywood, Tyler Perry earns somewhere in the neighborhood of $100 million a year. He was the first African-American to open his own studio, 200,000 square feet of sets and offices in Atlanta, Georgia. And all because he accumulated creative capital.

Just do it!

CREATE A SKETCH FOR *SATURDAY NIGHT LIVE*

"The perfect is the enemy of the good."
— ANSEL ADAMS, PHOTOGRAPHER

When I was a kid, my friends and I wrote skits for *Laugh-In*, the hottest show on TV. We even performed them for our parents. I played Edith Ann and that crazy telephone operator (one ringy-dingy) who stuffed Kleenex down her bra and you can bet your sweet bippie, we gave out Fickle Fingers of Fate.

Now, if we could do this when we were in seventh grade, surely you can do it now.

Your task this week is to write a sketch for *Saturday Night Live*. Maybe you'll even invite your friends to make one up, too, and stage your own *Saturday Night Live*.

Zumba for the Soul

- Play hopscotch with tape in the living room.
- Dress like a nun.
- Kiss five people.

You're in Good Company

Madeleine L'Engel's *A Wrinkle in Time* was rejected by 261 publishers.

WEEK 41

POOL TOYS

"Life is a closet filled with pool toys."

— AMY POEHLER, ACTRESS AND COMEDIAN

If you've read *E-Squared*, you might remember that I used affirmations to launch my freelance writing career. I even sent myself postcards with reminders that, "I, Pam Grout, am a great writer." "I, Pam Grout, have what it takes to sell to New York editors."

So I was thrilled to discover there's another writer out there who also used affirmations to kick off his career.

Scott Adams, the creator of the comic strip *Dilbert*, credits writing 15 affirmations a day ("I, Scott Adams, will be a famous cartoonist") for his meteoric rise.

Doing affirmations started as a lark. At the time, he was taking a hypnosis class. One of his classmates mentioned that by affirming what you want, you draw that very thing into your life. He didn't buy it at first, but figured, "What can it hurt? It's worth an experiment."

He started by getting a date with a girl who was clearly (at least in his mind) out of his league.

"At the time, I was a six, maybe a six-point-five. But she was a nine. The odds of her going out with me were long indeed," he said.

But after several weeks of affirming just that, they ended up dating.

Still not convinced, he decided to ask for investment tips. He wanted to play the stock market.

Of course, it would have helped if he actually knew how to buy stocks. But nevertheless, he began writing affirmations about his stock-buying prowess. He woke up one night and, with startling clarity, heard *Buy Chrysler*. He was a wet-behind-the-ears kid at the time and had no idea how to actually make the purchase.

But as he followed Chrysler (this was during the Lee Iacocca days), the stock shot straight up, filling its investors' pockets.

Next (and this time he was ready) he got a hint to invest in something called ASK computers. Sure enough, it quickly increased by 10, then 20 percent. Smugly, he sold it, happily pocketing the proceeds only to hear that it soon doubled and then tripled in value.

Next, he put his 15 affirmations a day to work on the GMAT test. He got a score of 77 the first time, which wasn't high enough to get into UC Berkeley, his graduate school of choice.

He decided he needed a 94 if he had any hope of securing admission to his dream school.

"I knew I wasn't really smart enough to get a 94, but I kept affirming and visualizing that number. I kept seeing a 94 peeking through that little window on the envelope," he says.

He retook the test, even though he knew 77 was probably his limit.

Several weeks passed before the envelope arrived in his mail slot. He turned it over, looked in that little window, and, you guessed it, his score was 94.

So by the time he began affirming that "I, Scott Adams, am a famous cartoonist," he was an old pro at affirmations. The universe had little choice but to reward him with the popular cartoon strip that, at last count, was syndicated in 2,000 newspapers around the world.

Just do it!

REIMAGINE A FAIRY TALE

"I used to be Snow White, but I drifted."
— MAE WEST, ACTRESS

They start with *Once Upon a Time* and end with *happily ever after*.

But what happens after the ill-fortuned couple reunites and rides off together into the sunset?

Disney has been reimagining fairy tales for nearly a century. Now it's your turn.

Anything goes. Here are some ideas:

1. Write it in modern times. Or not.

2. Make a sequel. What did Hansel and Gretel do when they grew up? Did Dorothy ever return to Oz?

3. Change the setting. What if that famous preindustrial European folktale happened in Chicago?

4. Superimpose fairy tales. What if Cinderella and Rapunzel met?

5. Add a twist. One swerve from the original plot can lead to all kinds of fascinating situations.

6. Tell it from a villain's viewpoint. The book *Wicked* and the Broadway musical it inspired is one such example.

7. Change the heroine into an "action princess."

Zumba for the Soul

- Learn to say *I love you* in five languages.
- Memorize three clean jokes.
- Feed a stranger's expired parking meter.

You're in Good Company

At the end of his career, Jackson Pollock couldn't work at all. He'd stare at his empty canvas and tell friends he "hated his easel, hated art."

SECTION FIVE

UPLIFTING THE WORLD

*"Artists are the gatekeepers of the truth.
It is our duty to be the voice of people who
are overlooked and marginalized."*

— COMMON, ACTOR AND PERFORMER

I thought this was a book about being an artist.

But as I let the muses speak, as I committed to being a channel, I noticed a second message bursting forth: that being creative is about imagining a new world, about designing a new vision.

Art, when done right, orchestrates healing.

As artists, we're out in the world conducting fieldwork on the culture.

Rather than protest and whine about the state of the world today, we must let our frustrations be our muse. We must let our disgruntlements inspire us to sing, to dance, to shout, "This is what we want instead."

When a hyacinth macaw loses its nest in the disappearing rainforest, it doesn't mope or call its therapist. It sings. It makes a joyful noise, reminding us what we have lost.

Ultimately, the world will be bound back together, not by politicians, but by thousands of individuals giving our gifts, thousands of individuals becoming ambassadors of the possible.

Our job is to put our art out there, to get others to gasp, weep, and hoot with joy. And only then, when their mouths are open, can we pop in the red pill.

Not only does art pry us open, but it encourages us to reach out, to join hands, to become a collective force for good. DIY doesn't mean doing it alone. Creating, after all, can be a team sport.

One person taps out a beat. Another leads into a melody, and before long, the entire audience has joined the chorus, raising hope for the whole world.

PUT IT IN A SONG

"We all collapse a little; may it be toward each other."
— RICHARD KENNEY, POET AND PROFESSOR

Every time there's a new mass shooting, I want to run to the bathroom, to vomit, to beat my fists against something hard and unyielding.

How could my country, the one I pledged allegiance to every morning for six years of grade school, have come to this?

Even though there is life to be lived today—this book to write, cookies to order for my finals-taking daughter—I feel drawn to these tragedies. I'm temped to sit comatose by the television set, watch the horror, and shake my head.

Yet, the squirrels still scamper up the tree to their nests, dutifully gathering acorns for the coming winter. They gather as loud humans barge in and out the door that's only feet from their measly food supply. They gather even though a huge storm last year sent their nest crashing to the ground below. They gather even though death is imminent and life can be cruel.

A part of me wants to hide, to take my daughter and flee to New Zealand, where her dad owns a winery and, presumably, a more peaceful existence.

But it's not a time to run away or to sit numb, helplessly devouring all the details.

It's a time to act, a time to create. A time for making peace out of chaos, a time for spinning love out of the threads of incomprehension.

It's easy for me to think, *How can I, one insignificant person from Kansas, stop a groundswell?*

But that's me forgetting who I am.

I am a creator, made in the image and likeness of the Great Creator.

And I am not insignificant.

If nothing else, I can write about what these massacres mean to me. I know nothing about Sandy Hook, really. Other than a short stint at a breathing program in nearby Washington, Connecticut, I have no real ties to this little town.

Yet, the story is also about me. It's about my anger, the many times I wanted revenge when someone rejected me. It's about the times I lashed out when someone said *good-bye* or *you're not what I'm looking for.*

It's about the unhealed places in all our hearts, those wounds that make us want to hit someone back.

Why do we want to strike out? Because we feel powerless. Because we have forgotten who we are. We have forgotten that the life force of the Creator thrums through our very veins.

It's easy to forget in this culture of convenience. No longer do we make our own bread, sing our own songs, dance our own jigs. No longer do we create much of anything. Too often we even forget that we can.

And in this forgetting, we lose our footing. Picasso said that when he realized painting was a way to give form to his terrors and his desires, he knew he had found his way.

The boy who killed at Sandy Hook had not yet found his way. He conned himself into believing he was insignificant. He didn't know that the life force of the entire universe pulsed through his body. He hadn't yet come to appreciate the sacredness of each moment.

He didn't know he could have screamed his rage and rejection into a song. He didn't know he could have danced his anger into a profound acceptance.

If only he had known.

It's too late for him. But it's not too late for us, all just as guilty of anger and rage as the killers we point fingers at.

You are powerful. You can create the answers to the horrors that confront our country, those things that make us want to throw up our hands, flee to foreign countries.

Inside you is a stage play that will inspire someone to forgive. Inside you is a painting or a story that can turn fear into hope, horror into peace. Even if it's peace in one person's heart, it is enough.

As Henry Miller once asked, "Where in this broad land is the holy of holies hidden?"

It's in the squirrels still gathering their acorns. It's in you.

Just do it!

ENJOY BEING A FLANEUR

"All truly great thoughts are conceived while walking."
— FRIEDRICH NIETZSCHE, PHILOSOPHER

Flaneur is French for *walker*. A flaneur doesn't walk to get somewhere. He walks to brazenly gawk and fall in love with the world. Not only is the act of walking revolutionary in a culture that relies so heavily on cars, but it retools the walker's psyche.

Many of the world's great thinkers were avid proponents of strolling, moseying, lollygagging. Beethoven walked every day, rain or shine. Dickens, Einstein, Darwin, Jobs, Thoreau, Aristotle, Beckett, and Tchaikovsky (one name is all it takes to identify these geniuses) were all daily walkers.

Zumba for the Soul

🎵 Tie-dye your underwear.

🎵 Make your own wrapping paper.

🎵 Read five children's books.

You're in Good Company

Before singer-songwriter Iris DeMent cut her first album, *Infamous Angel*, she worked at a Kmart in Nashville, Tennessee. Before she wrote her first song, she suffered the same self-doubt and insecurity that all of us do.

She'd write one line, tear it up, and convince herself it was useless since she'd never measure up to her heroes—Loretta Lynn, Merle Haggard, and the Carter Family.

WORKING ON BEHALF OF THE HEALING OF THE WORLD

"Is it naïve to seek constructive remedy with the likes of poetry and song from the voices of the people? I find it more foolish to seek lasting remedy with military power and a return to the status quo."

— KIM STAFFORD, POET AND WRITING TEACHER

During the holy month of Ramadan, in many Middle Eastern cities, a messenger called a *mesaharati* walks the empty alleyways just before dawn. His job is to bang drums, recite poetry, and wake people up for their morning prayer.

Artists are like mesaharatis, exploring the alleyways of the world, beating their drums, and waking people up.

They articulate a vision of how we, as individuals, as a society, might become more than what we are now. Utah Phillips used to call it exposing yourself to strangers.

Art serves humanity by:

1. **Smuggling new ideas into the culture.** It introduces people to new concepts, ideas that might not sit well coming from a politician or a pulpit. A good piece of art doesn't just move you. It rearranges you, shifts your internal tumblers.

   Jodi Picoult's novel *Small Great Things*, about an African-American pediatric nurse and the White Supremacist father who requests a different caretaker for his newborn, forced me to examine my own subtle prejudice and white privilege.

   Martin Luther King Jr., after hearing Pete Seeger's song "We Shall Overcome," turned it into one of the most powerful slogans of the civil rights movement.

   Or consider independent filmmaker John Sayles, who has invited his viewers to confront greed, injustice, poverty, and the environment.

   Artists are historians, storytellers, and keepers of an ancient wordless language based in love.

2. **Inspiring reverence.** Art rewires us to see the world differently, to love it more intimately. It slows us down, throws our senses wide open. It's a way to be wholly present, to see with new eyes.

It enables us to attend to and cherish previously invisible details. It helps us to see nature's infinitely overlooked enchantments, to notice the astonishing details of our everyday lives.

I'm often shocked at the details I've missed when I sit down and actually commit something to paper. One day I drew my daughter, Tasman, as she painted on the easel I gave her for Christmas. Drawing a five-year-old, by the way, is almost as challenging as drawing Mexican jumping beans. That's probably why painting students start with a still life.

As I began to draw the jeans she was wearing, I noticed the pointed pockets in the back, the double stitching down the seams, the rock she had picked up at the park and stuffed into her pocket. Before drawing, they were just a pair of brown jeans with an infuriating zipper that never stayed up. I found myself falling in love with those jeans and feeling even more love for the darling five-year-old who wore them.

3. **Keeping magic alive.** When his four-year-old daughter asked him what he did for his job, an art teacher explained that he taught people how to draw.

    She was aghast. "You mean, they forgot!"

    More accurately, they allowed their talent, their uniqueness, to be smothered by a long list of self-negating assumptions:

    "Oh, I could never do that."
    "People would think I'm stupid."

Think back to when you were a kid. The whole world was your palette. With one application of the imagination, Popsicle sticks turned into magical airplanes that did flips and flew upside down. A bar of soap was the Little Engine That Could (*"I think I can! I think I can!"*) or a limousine for a famous FBI spy. And the beach—oh, the beach—offered infinite building material. Remember the sand castle you built with moats, kings, ladies-in-waiting, and even a wizard? Back then, your imagination had no limits.

But then your parents piped in:

"Act your age."

"Don't talk with your mouth full."

"If everyone else stuck their head in a toilet, would you?"

And then teachers threw in their two cents:

"Paint between the lines."

"Make a cereal bowl like everybody else."

"Trees are green—not purple."

And then, just before you could do something really dangerous, your professors taught you about real art and literature, about metaphors and style. You finally realized how trivial your creative efforts were. After all, "Who are we compared to the great masters?"

At work, of course, it only got worse. Unless you were the boss—the big cheese—your main job was to follow the rules. Hold the imagination. Besides, with overtime hours, kids to feed, and a mortgage, you probably didn't have time to play with bars of soap and sand castles anyway.

Before long, you noticed you no longer knew how. Alas, life's colors had dimmed, its mysteries had run dry. Your capacity to wonder, to be surprised, to be puzzled, was long gone, buried in a box with your childhood Tinkertoys. Where's the remote control?

Some like to call this adulthood—being responsible.

I don't know about you, but I want to be carried away. I want to build sand castles, dance on tables, play hopscotch in my pajamas.

So what if society says these are useless pursuits, childish whims, total wastes of time?

So what if creativity doesn't guarantee security?

Creativity is unknown, even dangerous. But I'm tired of putting my chair in a row, marching in a straight line.

I'm ready to zig, to say *yes*, to make up my own dance.

Consider this your invitation to join me.

Just do it!

BECOME A THOUGHT ARTIST

"How wild a history is written within that bosom."
— EDGAR ALLAN POE, AUTHOR OF "THE RAVEN"

Sometimes it's hard to see the Oscar when you haven't so much as written the first "fade in." That's why you must be able to hold a vision in your mind's eye. You've got to be a thought artist. You've got to choose what's trending in your life.

Forget the facts. The fact that you've never written a screenplay, the fact that you're not even sure how far in to indent the first character's name.

Focus on that little gold statue sitting on your fireplace mantle. Focus on the applause as you go up to nervously give your acceptance speech.

Shirley MacLaine, who won best actress for her role as Aurora Greenway in *Terms of Endearment*, is a master thought artist. She saw herself getting an Oscar long before the March awards ceremony. She even pictured the dress she would wear.

Zumba for the Soul

- Make up a character and create a Facebook profile for him or her.

- Write a press release about yourself.

- Carry an idea catcher (for me, it's a notebook) wherever you go.

You're in Good Company

Lin-Manuel Miranda, creator of the smash hit *Hamilton*, admitted, "Anytime I write something, I go through the 'I'm a fraud' phase. I go through the 'I'll never finish' phase."

CREATE OR DIE

"What can we gain by sailing to the moon if we are not able to cross the abyss that separates us from ourselves. This is the most important of all voyages of discovery and without it all the rest are not only useless but disastrous."

— THOMAS MERTON, TRAPPIST MONK

In the next hour, 60 people in the United States will attempt to kill themselves. Four of them will be successful. By the time you finish reading this chapter, one of your fellows will be dead—not from cancer, not from a worn-out heart, but from the unbearable burden of his own pain, the weight of which finally convinced him to place a gun to his precious temple or a razor blade to the wrist that his own mother held as she taught him to walk.

The World Health Organization estimates that by 2030, depression will outpace cancer, stroke, war, and accidents as the leading cause of disability and death.

I shouldn't have to point out that something is wrong—foot-stompingly wrong—with this picture.

Something sacred has been violated. The human soul has lost faith.

Slowly, over time, we have given up our inheritance. We have turned over our power to think for ourselves, to make things up, to imagine, to plan, to dream. Instead, we grab our phones, reach for our remotes. We call Pizza Hut.

Inside each and every one of us is a master chef, an inventor, a writer, a statesman. All these heroes, these immense giants that exist within our souls, are literally dying from boredom. They're sick to death of streaming Hulu.

Convenience food, streaming television, and ready-made everything is holding hostage the gods within us. It's no wonder we're all depressed. We, the greatest of all creators, with the capability to build cities and inspire nations, are squandering our time watching reruns of *Sex and the City*.

We have forgotten that whole galaxies exist within our grasp. Our deepest impulse is to create. Without it, life becomes sterile, little but rote recitation.

I'm not fool enough to suggest that something as simple as writing a poem or singing a song will change the suicide rate in this country. I'm not proposing that we trade in our Prozac for sketchbooks.

But it's a start.

The very act of creating is an act of power, an act of hope. It's a reminder that we are not powerless pawns, not cattle in a big cosmic slaughterhouse. Writing a song or drawing a vase of freshly picked delphiniums is a reminder that we can do something, a reminder that we have the power to make something from nothing. And as those reminders add up, as hope begins to grow, we no longer feel overwhelmed by our troubles, by the troubles of the world. We remember that we, as humans, as cocreators with the universe, have immense power to change things.

It is our responsibility to bear witness to the pulse and beauty of life. Our only job is to discover and sing our own song.

You can either answer the summons. Or you can die.

Just do it!

ACT OUT A SCENE FROM *THE WIZARD OF OZ*

"Take your broken heart. Make it into art."

— CARRIE FISHER, ACTRESS
WHO PLAYED PRINCESS LEIA

Yes, you're going to need friends. Somebody's got to be the Tin Man, the Scarecrow, and the Cowardly Lion. Maybe you'll even want a Toto and a Wicked Witch. You pick the scene. You pick the cast. Remember, however, that this week you're an actor, a singer, and maybe even a wizard.

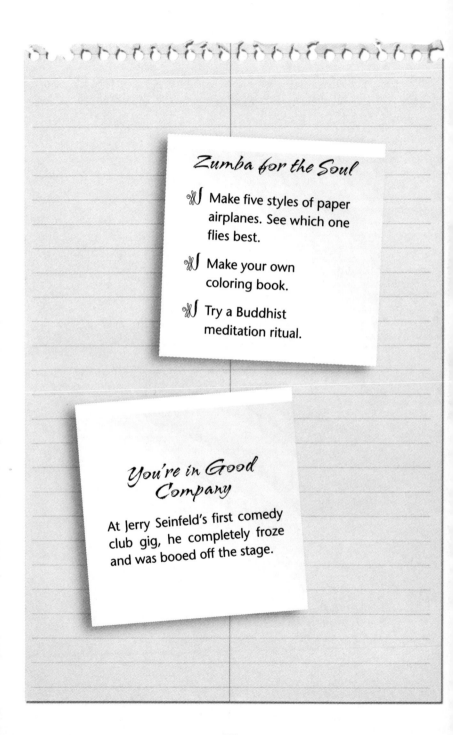

Zumba for the Soul

- Make five styles of paper airplanes. See which one flies best.

- Make your own coloring book.

- Try a Buddhist meditation ritual.

You're in Good Company

At Jerry Seinfeld's first comedy club gig, he completely froze and was booed off the stage.

WHAT DOES THE UNIVERSE WANT TO SAY THROUGH YOU?

"Without you, the rest of us are without a source of many wonderful things."

— LEO BUSCAGLIA, PROFESSOR AND
AUTHOR OF MANY BESTSELLERS ON LOVE

A local physician once prescribed a friend of mine "an hour of beauty a day." She was suffering from chronic fatigue, a condition with no underlying medical condition. He ordered her to go out and, every day, spend no less than 60 minutes witnessing generosity, grace, and artistry.

This is also the starting line for creators. We must begin with a sense of abundance, knowing we are, as Buscaglia told us, the source of something wonderful.

All pleasure in creating begins with this sense of unlimited possibility. In recognizing that treasures are everywhere. Our job is to gather them up and give them voice.

An artist is someone who reveals important things on behalf of the world, someone who, as poet Mary Oliver tells us, pays attention, is astonished, and tells us about it.

Being an artist is not a cheap way to get attention. An artist is offering a gift to the world and to every being in it.

So what if no one wants to buy it? Staple it to a telephone pole. Send it out in a blog. Give generously. Squander everything.

Dreams get away if we don't tell them or write them down.

In the history of the universe, there is never going to be another you. Your experiences, your wisdom, your gifts can never be replicated. You have something that the world will never be able to access without you.

Every person has a unique perspective. Every person has gold to offer. Don't cheat us of your contribution.

Jolie Guillebeau, an artist from Portland, Oregon, says it was a full year after graduating from art school before she was able to claim her chosen profession. "Despite the degree, I couldn't call myself an artist. I couldn't paint or draw—not even one picture. I was paralyzed by fear, perfectionism, and the internal judge that came onboard during art school."

After four months of scribbling in her journal, she came up with a succinct summary of what she believed. It contained two words.

Painters paint.

"I knew I had to paint. I knew I had to believe in the abundance of ideas. So I committed to painting one painting a day for three months whether I had a good idea or not. It was the only way I knew to face down my gremlins, one day at a time."

After 100 days, she finished 100 paintings. Miraculously, she even sold 87 of them.

Six years later, she's still painting a picture a day. She sees it as her way of sharing her story, sharing her abundance.

Find your abundance in the little moments that deserve celebration, even if no one but you notices.

Just do it!

WRITE A LETTER TO THE EDITOR

"Leave the world more interesting for your being here."
— NEIL GAIMAN, BRITISH AUTHOR

There's something that really bugs you, something that's been eating at you for months. Instead of silently stewing, now's the time to give your two cents' worth. Who knows? The editor might even print it.

Zumba for the Soul

- Find a tree to decorate (à la Christmas) in the park.

- Pull something out of the trash and make something with it.

- Don a piece of clothing that doesn't really "fit" the dress code.

You're in Good Company

Stevie Nicks gets so nervous before going onstage that she can't even apply makeup. She shakes hard and gets sick to her stomach. While she considers herself a decent songwriter, she persists in her belief that she's not a very good musician.

INNER WILD CHILD

"Never ask whether you can do something. Say instead that you are doing it. Then fasten your seat belt."

— JULIA CAMERON, AUTHOR OF *THE ARTIST'S WAY*

For years, we've been advised to get in touch with our inner child. We've been told that the only way to heal our core emotional issues is to embrace our inner child, to make him or her our most trusted confidante.

The only problem is we forget to ask her about the tea party with the fairy king. We spent so much time getting her to talk about her father that was never there for her and about the daycare worker who locked her in the closet that we failed to get her to share her crazy jig, her beautiful song, her wild fantasies.

Kids know important things, things we mature grown-ups have forgotten. Kids know that mud puddles are for sailing sticks, that snowstorms are for making angels, and that broken broomsticks are really prancing ponies. They know Skittles are better than money and that finding a pretty seashell is an important way to spend the day.

And when it comes to making art, it never occurs to a first grader he might not know how to paint, how to dance, or how to sculpt. After all, Play-Doh can be made into anything. Kids know how to dream big dreams, how to make friends with dragons and princes and elves.

This is the inner child we want to consult.

Not only do we want to call back that inner wild child, the one who climbs trees and builds sand castles, but we want to do the things kids do.

Like show-and-tell. Why isn't this a normal thing? Every week or so we should get together with families, our closest friends, and show them something we really like, something unique about us. We should bring in some doodle we made on the side of a Visa bill or something we thought up while waiting at the dry cleaner.

Adults still think things up. We just don't tell anyone. We don't think it's important. Not with lawns that need mowing and mufflers that need fixing.

How much closer we'd all be if we stopped long enough to honor one another in a circle of show-and-tell? If we listened to one another's stories, looked at one another's creations. We're all hungry for community. We need more ways to connect. Adults still need show-and-tell. Literally.

We also still need story time, music time, nap time, and snack time. Probably even more than kids.

Preschoolers get to play the tambourine, sing silly songs, and dance in wild circles while we watch from the sidelines as proper adults.

Whatever happened to hanging finger paintings on our refrigerator? Giving book reports? Playing charades?

Instead of focusing on inner child processing, on inner child work, I see communities of people forming circles to show off their self-portraits, their *Art & Soul* badges, their balloon sculptures. I see them laughing at their various adventures, leaving poems on sidewalks, and spray painting grand statements on bridges. I see a big potluck with everyone sampling the staggering variety of sandwiches they created. I see celebrations of newly invented holidays, variety shows with skits and homemade instruments.

But most of all, I see healing, fun, life as it is for a six-year-old.

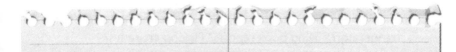

Just do it!

HOST A SHOW-AND-TELL

"You are here to localize a cosmic celebration."

— MICHAEL BECKWITH, POWERFUL
NEW THOUGHT TEACHER

Remember the essay "All I Really Need to Know I Learned in Kindergarten"? Well, the reason it was so popular is because it struck a chord. What else, really, do we need to know?

This week, invite your friends over. Ask them to bring something they value. Take turns sharing. You'll be amazed at how much you've missed Show-and-Tell.

Zumba for the Soul

🖎 Write a new ending to a mystery novel.

🖎 Impersonate your favorite cartoon character.

🖎 Host a Barbra Streisand or Keanu Reeves (or your choice) film festival.

You're in Good Company

Tom Wolfe, best-selling author of such books as *The Electric Kool-Aid Acid Test* and *The Bonfire of the Vanities*, says, "The awful thing about the first sentence of any book is that as soon as you've written it you realize this piece of work is not going to be the great thing that you envision. It can't be."

WEEK 47

COURAGE

"You need a certain amount of nerve, an almost physical nerve, the kind you need to walk a log across a river."

— MARGARET ATWOOD,
CANADIAN POET AND AUTHOR

Being creative is an act of great daring.

Every time we write or sing or paint, we put ourselves in jeopardy. We step out on the highwire with a whole circus tent of people watching.

It's no wonder we often chicken out.

Doing your art covers damned near everything—your need to be visible, your need to tell the truth, your need to make a difference.

Is it any wonder you're just a slight bit anxious?

Often, our fear shows up in disguise—as procrastination ("I'll work on scene three tomorrow"), being too busy ("I'll start the novel when the kids get in school"), or depression ("I'll start painting when I'm not so blue").

Call it what you will, it's all the same issue.

Being creative is genuinely spooky.

As much as people idolize movie stars and best-selling authors who appear on *Good Morning America*, they don't really applaud the people in their own lives who hole themselves up to write poems or practice the guitar. When we create, we're often alone, transported to another world, a world that doesn't always include those within elbow distance. People sometimes feel threatened.

They'll say *ride on* and *you, go, girl* when you get something published or land a part in a play, but until that time, they tend to cast aspersive looks your way.

When you create, you make yourself vulnerable, throw prudence to the wind, hold nothing back.

As long as you keep your mouth shut, nod your head at the right time, follow the prescribed do's and don'ts, nobody's going to laugh, disagree, or scrutinize.

But once you write, say, or paint something, the masks come off. People are going to know. And that takes courage with a capital C.

It also takes courage to joust with your own terrors, to confront your own truths. When you surrender to your art, you may just find your truth contrasts with the persona you present to the world.

You might find out that, God forbid, you don't really want to do what society thinks you should. Emily Dickinson, for example, discovered through her poetry that she didn't really want to marry and keep house like her mother.

And it especially takes courage to stand up to those buggery little voices that keep telling you you're boring, the ones that insist if you write or paint, you're risking financial failure.

It takes courage to rail against them, to forge ahead when they keep sticking their leg out, trying to trip you.

It takes courage to keep going when your work doesn't meet your expectations, when instead of getting Jane Austen, you get Barney's sing-along. You've got to keep plodding ahead anyway.

There's a lot of rejection, a lot of times people are going to say, "Sorry, I don't want it."

We must be courageous enough to forge ahead anyway.

Just do it!

CHOREOGRAPH A DANCE

*"I am secretary to a wisdom the
world has made available to me."*

— **KIM STAFFORD**, WRITING TEACHER

Okay, so you're not George Balanchine, and the only dance
step you know is "put your right foot in." That doesn't matter.
Put on a favorite piece of music, get up, and express yourself.

Zumba for the Soul

- Stage a *Monopoly* tournament.

- Anonymously send your
  favorite poem to 20 people.

- Dress in a sexy costume (or
  something unlike you) and go
  out for a night on the town.

You're in Good Company

Bob Dylan was hooted off the
stage the first time he performed with an electric guitar.

TEA FOR TWO

"There is only one real deprivation . . . and that is not to be able to give one's gifts to those one loves most."

— MAY SARTON, POET AND MEMOIRIST

Once you're tapped in (and I guarantee you'll get juice if you follow the other two practices), you're going to want to cross-pollinate with other artists. And I don't mean on Facebook, although that is certainly a noble goal. I'm thinking salon, as in French salons of the 17th and 18th centuries. Get a group together with the sole purpose of sharing your muses' offerings.

Just as the salons of earlier ages brought about what we now call the Age of Enlightenment, I'm counting on the salons generated by this book to uplift this sad and stormy world, to jar us out of our annoying ruts. FYI: this is not some small thing I'm asking you to do.

Salons, from ancient Greek symposia to Gertrude Stein's famous Paris get-togethers, have always been the incubators of provocative—dare I say dangerous—ideas. Passionate conversation leads to passionate action. I expect nothing less than greatness.

This is a good thing. If you're like me, you have a burning desire to leap out of ruts, right?

Even though the universe always guides us, always helps us create, sometimes we need someone more human to remind us. That's why it's vital to find an environment where art is valued and art-making is encouraged.

This week, you're going to find an art partner, someone you can talk to about your artistic goals, fears, and accomplishments. Someone who is willing to hear what you have to say, a special soul mate who is genuinely interested in the thoughts and feelings sashaying through your soul.

The person who wins this coveted position (and this is a highly sought-after position) is going to be "rah-rah-rah-ing" you every week. They're going to believe in you, encourage you, pat you on the back for faithfully showing up and doing your art.

If you feel a little funny asking someone for this much time, remember you are offering a gift. Not only will you be doing the same thing for them (listening, seeing, and rah-rah-ing their art-making), but you are offering your beautiful self.

This person gets the privilege of seeing the real you. Not the you who got the shoplifting conviction in junior high or the you who flunked out of sixth grade. Those are petty things that you did as a human.

No, this person is getting a ringside seat to the richer, deeper, God you. And that, my friend, is a rare and priceless gift. Witnessing the authentic, godlike side of a person always raises the person who witnesses it to a higher level.

Oftentimes, we show up to our friends and family as our little selves, the selves that obsess, the selves that eat too much sugar. But the *big* you, the artist you that is willing to stand naked and unafraid, gives nothing but gifts. Trust me! You will inspire your partner. And she will be glad you asked.

Maybe you already know someone who is willing to play this part in your budding new artistic career. If not, post a sign at the local theater or library or hobby shop. Run a personals ad. Someone is out there.

It's probably better to choose someone you're not already in a rut with—like your husband or your best friend. No offense, but familiar relationships tempt us to stay in our ruts. These get-togethers are meant to be fresh, raw, and alive.

I could give you a list of rules on how to do it, but I trust that just like doing art opens you to a deeper knowing, this process of meeting and sharing with your partner will happen naturally, too.

I suggest just two commitments. First, gather every week. It may seem like a pain—carving out space in your already-bulging day-timer. But eventually there will be nothing more important.

Rule number two: Never judge or critique each other's work. Yes, show each other your work—proudly, boldly—but never make comments or suggestions. You are here to change the story from "it has to be good" to "you did it"!

Your job is to cheer and carry on about the fact your partner showed up and did the work. Period. That is all that is important. Showing up. Doing the work. The muses will take care of the rest.

Just do it!

CREATE AND POST A NOTICE.

*"Something moved from background to foreground
that day. A dream took one big step closer."*

— JEN LEE, ARTIST AND FILMMAKER

W.S.A. (white, single artist) seeks rainbow-colored partner. The exact wording doesn't matter. Just make a poster, a notice, or an ad, and post it on the bulletin board of your local theater, library, or hobby shop.

You can find the nearest Sharpie and write something like this: *Audacious but reverent artist seeks audacious, but reverent art partner. Call_____(name)_____at_____ (phone)_____*

Or you can design your own. Something that shouts bold, audacious, irreverent.

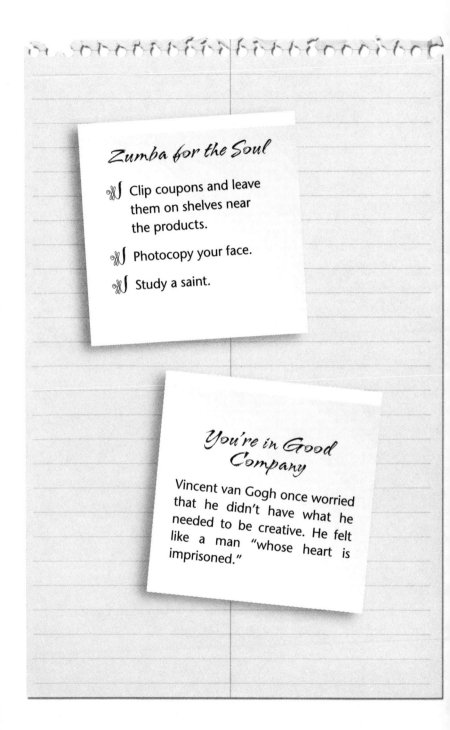

Zumba for the Soul

- Clip coupons and leave them on shelves near the products.
- Photocopy your face.
- Study a saint.

You're in Good Company

Vincent van Gogh once worried that he didn't have what he needed to be creative. He felt like a man "whose heart is imprisoned."

A LITTLE HELP FROM OUR FRIENDS

"Cluster together like stars."

— HENRY MILLER, AUTHOR

Mary Shelley, who was barely 20 when she wrote the classic tale *Frankenstein*, claimed she'd have never done it without the encouragement of friends who were staying together at a villa in Lake Geneva, Switzerland. It was a dreary, rainy summer and Shelley and friends, including her future husband, Percy Bysshe Shelley, and the poet Lord Byron, wiled away long days in front of a log fire. Mary, egged on by her poet comrades who challenged one another to write a ghost story, decided to join the fun. She put her mind to work until, one night, the muses woke her up with a horrifying tale of the now-familiar young doctor and his unorthodox science experiment.

Mary Shelley may not have been alert enough to catch the story if she hadn't been around others with an artistic vision.

Artists need comrades who can hold the high watch, who can say *bravo* when they want to say *I quit.*

The myth of the lonely, long-suffering artist exacts a high price. We don't have to be alone and, in fact, can nourish each other's creativity when we peek out of our isolated artist's garrets to say, "Hi!"

From time immemorial, artists have gathered in cafes to share ideas, grouse about editors, trade tips on the best place to buy paint. Hemingway's little black book included Gertrude Stein, F. Scott Fitzgerald, Matisse, and many other well-known artists.

Maxine Kumin and Anne Sexton, both Pulitzer Prize–winning poets, had special phone lines installed in their homes so they could critique each other's work. As fledgling poets, they first met at a poetry class at the Boston Center for Adult Education. They went on to form an informal poetry group that met biweekly in members' homes. Whenever Kumin's children saw her setting out the cups and glasses, they always protested, "Oh, no. Not the poets again. We'll never get any sleep."

When the chemistry's right, artists' get-togethers can be loud and exciting. One person's ideas inspire another's. Each contributes his or her piece to make something larger.

Within the first year, four of the five members of their poetry group published books.

Pulitzer Prize winner Tony Kushner said the idea that he alone wrote *Angels in America* was pure rubbish. Actors, directors, former lovers, friends, and even one-night stands all left their traces in his play's text. "It's fiction that artists labor in isolation and that artistic accomplishment is exclusively the provenance of individual talents," he said.

Art, rather than isolating us as it's so mythically portrayed, actually brings us together.

When we share our work, it binds us closer. We reveal ourselves to one another. When we read a poem or show a painting, we find kindred spirits, head-nodding friends who say, "Yeah, me, too. That's just how I feel."

We all want to connect, to be close.

Lately, however, we've learned to connect through what medical intuitive Caroline Myss calls "woundology." I tell you my dad wasn't there for me, that I used to date an alcoholic, and that I'm a recovering codependent and, boy, do we have a landslide of conversation.

Only problem is that from now on, we'll deal with each other with kid gloves. Don't stand me up because then I'll be reminded of my dad and I'll have to be really sad and reject you and blah, blah, blah, blah, blah.

Yeah, we're connected, but is it the kind of connection that really nurtures a friendship? What I'd like to propose is a much better way to connect.

Let's tell each other our deepest dreams. Let's read each other the poems we've secretly written. Let's pretend you're Mark Ruffalo and I'm Nicole Kidman, and let's go out and chow strawberry shortcake.

Sure, we're still going to bump up against occasional anger and angst, but if we channel those burning emotions into a character, a short story, a song, we get it out and let it go. By turning it into something tangible and real, something we can share with another human being, we are free to release it.

Talking about a problem is fine. Everyone needs to feel that someone cares, that someone is listening. But when

you turn your anxiety into a something—a story, a poem—
it becomes concrete and you suddenly own it instead of it
owning you.

I'm tired of leading with my weaknesses, hoping maybe
you'll like me because I'm insecure or scared. Yeah, I've
thought about taking a razor blade to my arm. I've also got-
ten down on my hands and knees and begged a man not to
leave me. But I'm also a dancing goddess, a twirling master
who longs to dance with the God in you.

Just do it!

COMPOSE A POEM

"Nobody gets talker's block."

— SETH GODIN, BLOGGER EXTRAORDINAIRE

It might help to put on a red beret. Or grow one of those shaggy beards. Get into the spirit of it. Create a rhyming poem, a haiku, or a poem that expresses your frustrations. Just make sure you write something.

On the next page, you'll find a poem I wrote, my take on the popular Dr. Seuss book *Green Eggs and Ham*. If nothing else, it should eliminate any frustrations about not being good enough or not knowing how to do it. I had never written a poem when I wrote this for one of my creativity classes.

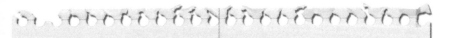

Green Eggs and Pam

I am Pam.
Pam, I am.

I did not like that Pam, I am.
Who always said, "yes, sir," "yes, ma'am."

I did not like that Pam, I am.
I did not like "yes, sir," "yes, ma'am."

I longed to step out of my box.
To dance, to scream, to be a fox.

I did not like "yes sir," "yes, ma'am."
I did not like them.
Pam, I am.

But would I? Could I?
Break the bars?
Would I? Could I? Reach the stars?

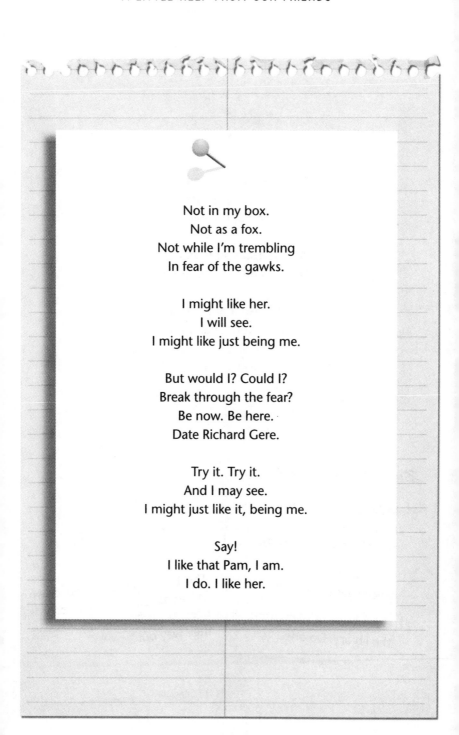

Not in my box.
Not as a fox.
Not while I'm trembling
In fear of the gawks.

I might like her.
I will see.
I might like just being me.

But would I? Could I?
Break through the fear?
Be now. Be here.
Date Richard Gere.

Try it. Try it.
And I may see.
I might just like it, being me.

Say!
I like that Pam, I am.
I do. I like her.

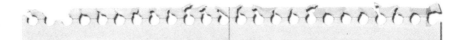

I even like her when in pain.
And in the dark.
And in the rain.

And as a star. And up a tree.
She is so me, so me, you see.

I do so like that Pam, I am.
Thank you. Thank you.

Pam, I am.

Zumba for the Soul

- Make a certificate (for best joke-teller?, best sport?) and give it away.

- Leave entertaining voicemails for friends.

- Get a book of spells from the library. Do one.

You're in Good Company

The Beatles were turned down by producers at Decca Records because "guitar groups were on their way out."

A PROUD TRIBE

*"And yet they, who passed away long ago,
still exist in us, as predisposition, as burden upon
fate, as murmuring blood, and as gesture
that rises up from the depths of time."*

— RAINER MARIA RILKE, AUSTRIAN POET

Becoming an artist is a little like joining the Lions Club. The secret password is "I want to be more." The secret handshake is "I believe."

The only dues are the ones you pay to yourself, the time you set aside to be alone and to listen. The initiation is the agreement to see something bigger, to delve deeper when convention says that's all there is. While others try to close the book, the artist opens it, says there are more pages possible.

To say *yes* to the muse that whispers ever-so-quietly in your ear is a sacred covenant. To say *here I am* to any art form is to join a powerful brotherhood.

It's to come face-to-face with Rumi and Shakespeare, to put on the cloak of Gauguin, Gilda Radner, Peter Gabriel. It's to join a proud circle with many members of all places and times.

Go to these brothers and sisters of yours, these kindred spirits, and study their ways, learn from their successes and failures, and then add your quota. They have left stones for you to step on, footsteps to follow. Do not worry that you have nothing new or original to add.

Before Beethoven began scoring 500 songs a year, he studied under his hero, Joseph Haydn. Eric Clapton followed the lead of John Lee Hooker, B.B. King, and Buddy Guy. Of course, now he's gone on to inspire legends of musicians making music today.

"I often feel I've been handed something to carry on. I feel a strong sense of responsibility. It's like carrying a torch," Eric Clapton says.

At first, we might copy the torch of our heroes, even emulate their style. Imitation is natural and necessary to the beginning artist. Even young Picasso painted in the style of his contemporaries for the first few years of his budding career.

Eventually, however, when we stand long enough in the commitment, our own style and voice step forward.

One of the lessons I cherish most comes from John Steinbeck's *Working Days: The Journal of* The Grapes of Wrath. It's a diary from 1939, detailing the excruciating self-doubt and despair he experienced during the novel's writing process.

Keep in mind that *The Grapes of Wrath* won the Pulitzer Prize and provided the foundation for Steinbeck's Nobel Prize two decades later. Keep in mind that Steinbeck managed to write a whopping 27 books.

Although he strictly forbade this revelatory memoir from being made public during his lifetime, I'm forever glad he relented to release it after his death. This powerful diary offers a glimpse into Steinbeck's daily thought process, showing us a deeply reassuring record of a flawed but committed creator.

What follows are short excerpts from the diary of a writer, widely regarded today as a genius, who suffered from the same imposter syndrome as the rest of us:

"My many weaknesses are beginning to show their heads. I'm not a writer. I've been fooling myself and other people."

"I am assailed with my own ignorance and inability."

"No one else knows my lack of ability the way I do. I am pushing against it all the time."

"This book has become a misery to me because of my inadequacy."

"It's just a run-of-the-mill book. And the awful thing is that it is absolutely the best I can do."

Um, run of the mill? *The Grapes of Wrath* won two of literature's most lauded accolades.

Steinbeck's diary is an important creative scripture for those of us laboring in the arts. It's a reminder that the only quality that sets the brilliant apart from the mediocre is the willingness to let doubt happen and plow forward anyway.

I encourage you to stand on the shoulders of John Steinbeck and other artists who have gone before you. Take their hands and let them help you across the chasm.

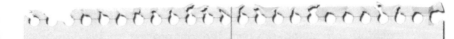

Just do it!

DESIGN THE COVER OF YOUR MEMOIR

"Art enables us to find ourselves
and lose ourselves at the same time."
— THOMAS MERTON, AMERICAN MONK

Maybe you just want a full-size shot of your face with the title of your book embedded in your front left tooth. Maybe you'd rather show your scrapbook from sixth grade or the first-place trophy you won that summer in the gunny sack race.

What color will your book cover be? Will it have lots of words? A fancy subtitle? You're the designer. What best represents you to the rest of the world?

Zumba for the Soul

- ❀ Create a billboard for Times Square.
- ❀ Send a tweet to your Congressman.
- ❀ Take a selfie with someone you've never met.

You're in Good Company

Teachers of opera singer Enrico Caruso said he had no voice at all and could not sing. His parents encouraged him to be an engineer.

CELEBRATING LIFE

*"I do wish to run, to seize this greatest time in
all the history of man to be alive, stuff my senses with it,
eye it, touch it, listen to it, smell it, taste it, and hope
that others will run with me, pursuing and pursued
by ideas and idea-made machines."*

— RAY BRADBURY, PROLIFIC
SCIENCE FICTION AUTHOR

How long has it been since you've danced? Be honest now.
I'm talking about really dancing where the beat and your
body become one. Where you surrendered to the rhythm and
lost all sense of time.

When was the last time you sang a song? Or skipped. Or
laughed, for that matter?

In *Divine Secrets of the Ya-Ya Sisterhood*, the Ya-Yas, four
lifelong friends, survived divorce, alcoholism, even death by

using humor and a sense of joy in the details of their lives. In the whole scheme of things, their lives were pretty ordinary. None were famous or had earth-shattering careers. None were millionaires or known outside their little burg of Thornton, Alabama. But boy, did these ladies know how to live. They turned their ordinary lives into something extraordinary. They didn't just fix dinner. They prepared feasts. They didn't just throw parties. They hosted galas.

That's what being creative is all about. It's more than just making a painting or submitting a poem. It's about making a life.

Look up the word *creativity* in the dictionary and you'll find a picture, to borrow an old Rodney Dangerfield joke, of my friend Michelle. She doesn't write (except for Christmas cards in January) or paint, but everything she does is done with joie de vivre, a sense of sparkle. In her kitchen, for example, she posted a picture of a fierce dragon with these words: "Mom without coffee." She stages a Monty Python film festival every February, makes Vegas-worthy costumes, and throws parties where everyone comes naked except for raincoats.

She's a kindred spirit to Dame Edith Sitwell, who said, "I am not eccentric. I'm just more alive than most people. I am an electric eel in a pond of goldfish."

The vast majority of adults in this country have become goldfish. They've turned their joy thermostats way down. Having fun is just too much trouble. They're trying to save energy. What they don't realize is joy and fun actually create energy.

Next time you're at an airport, notice what happens when a flight gets canceled. Children barely notice. They play hopscotch, impersonate Elsa from the Disney movie *Frozen*, crawl under their seats. Only their seats are not seats. They're haunted houses or castles or magic playrooms.

Adults just sit there, staring at their phones.

Every day, we have 1,440 minutes. We can either waste those precious minutes looking at our phones or we can turn ourselves into electric eels.

Just do it!

GET OUT THE WATERCOLORS

"The creative process is not controlled by a switch you can simply turn on or off; it's with you all the time."

— ALVIN AILEY, DANCER

I don't want to hear it. So what if you haven't painted since you were in fifth grade? So what if you don't own any watercolors? Buy a children's set at Walmart for $1.29. Paint on typing paper or a cardboard box. This is meant to be fun.

Zumba for the Soul

- Design an invitation to your first sculpture show.

- Rearrange your furniture.

- Read *Random Acts of Kindness*. Do three of them.

You're in Good Company

Famous French film director François Truffaut was a movie critic for years because he was too afraid to direct his own films.

THE ONLY BOOK THAT WILL CHANGE YOUR LIFE IS THE ONE YOU WRITE YOURSELF

"And yes, I said, Yes, I will, yes."

— JAMES JOYCE, IRISH WRITER

Operating manual for being an artist.

a) Get a 99-cent notebook. In August, during back-to-school sales, I get them four for a buck.

b) Get a pen. You can easily steal one from any bank.

With these simple tools, you can sketch a masterpiece, pen a poem, write next year's Oscar-nominated screenplay. The tools themselves are irrelevant. What matters is being available, being the pipeline through which creativity can flow.

You don't need to know a damned thing going in. Uncertainty, despite what you've been taught, is a virtue.

Nor do you need to perfect any particular technique. Once an art form becomes a technique, it loses its freshness, its sense of adventure. It becomes a business.

Passion, love, that burning fire within your soul will create your art.

Give up all resistance to looking stupid. Embrace mistakes and surprises. Be willing to strike out into unknown territory.

In other words, you gotta pick up the pen. You gotta begin. Ideas only come when you act.

Persistence, daily attendance to the muse, as Steinbeck showed us, is the best predictor of quality.

I love this story from the book *Art & Fear* which, in my humble opinion, says it all.

A ceramics professor, at the beginning of the semester, divided his students into two groups. The first was to be graded solely on quantity of output. Grades could be measured on a bathroom scale. Students who completed 50 pots, for example, would get an A, those who made 40 a B, and so on. The second group was required to make but one pot, albeit a perfect one. Grades would be meted out on quality alone.

A funny thing happened. By the end of the semester, not only were the one-pot students frazzled with anxiety, but their pots, the alleged masterpieces they'd been laboring over for four long months, weren't the best.

The students who spun pots, one after another, ended up with the works of the highest quality. Rather than sit around theorizing about the best methods, these students simply practiced, practiced, learned from their mistakes, and practiced some more.

If you simply start, if you simply move, you can figure out how to do most anything. The technical aspects of creativity (say, the formatting, the mixing of colors, the lighting) make up less than 10 percent of any creative endeavor. The other 90-plus percent comes from practice, from surrender, from something that's much bigger than you.

Don't be afraid of making bad things. Be afraid of making nothing at all.

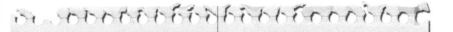

Just do it!

DO A STREET PERFORMANCE

*"Art would be my shield and honesty my spear
and to hell with Jack and his close-set eyes."*
— MAYA ANGELOU, AUTHOR OF MANY BOOKS

Okay, so just what is a performance piece? For one thing, you could dress like Elvis and go dancing. You could paint yourself blue and do mime in the park. I saw a human jukebox once in San Francisco. Well, actually it was a refrigerator box decorated like a jukebox. The guy inside sang requests depending on which slot you put your dollar through.

You can make a drum from an old wastebasket or shakers with beans and empty soda bottles. Maybe you'll invent a new type of performance, like the Andean musicians who made shakers out of goat's toenails and a string instrument from an armadillo shell. Remember, anything is possible.

If you'd prefer, go to an open mic or a karaoke bar.

Zumba for the Soul

- Learn to say *hi!* in sign language.

- Go to a restaurant in a part of town you've never been.

- Make a list of 100 things to do before you die.

You're in Good Company

Even after winning four Academy Awards, two Emmys, three Golden Globes, and being knighted in his home country of Great Britain, Laurence Olivier admitted, "Stage fright is still waiting outside the door, any door, waiting to get you. It can come at any time, in any form."

❦ AFTERWORD ❦

THE CREATIVE LIFE

"Each second we live in a new and unique moment of the universe, a moment that never was before and will never be again."

— PABLO CASALS, CELLIST

Some of you picked up this book in the hopes it will jump-start a particular artistic career. Maybe you want to be a writer or an actor or take on some other predefined creative path. While that's a noble goal, and I applaud and send you all the best juju for limitless success, I'd also like to point out that the real goal of this book is to leap hard and fast away from everything you think you know.

Living a creative life has nothing to do with a particular career. It's about infusing creativity and employing imagination, inventiveness, and playfulness into everything you do.

Every minute of your life provides an opportunity for creativity. Whether you're parenting, making a sales call, or shaking your tail feather on the Zumba floor.

Creativity is a mind-set—a scrappy, damn-the-torpedoes way of approaching your day.

You don't need to know anything. You just have to begin.

Throw off the shackles of the past. Say *no* to the petty trinkets, the measly hoops you've been jumping through.

Pablo Casals, the famous cellist, once asked, "What do we teach our children in school? We teach them that two and two makes four, and that Paris is the capital of France. When will we also teach them what they are?

"We should say to each of them: You are a marvel. You are unique. In all the world there is no other child exactly like you. In the millions of years that have passed there has never been a child like you. You have the capacity for anything."

That's why the creative life is a sacred calling. Uncork the champagne. Roll out the gold-glittered streamers. We've come to grow the holy vision of God.

⁂ ACKNOWLEDGMENTS ⁑

Mad props to all my readers who delight me every day with emails and kind words. Thanks, as always, to my possibility posses (you know who you are), to Jim Dick and Tasman Grout, to Melanie Loyd, and to my fellow creators and editors at Hay House. I am so blessed.

ABOUT THE AUTHOR

Pam Grout has served as an extra in a zombie movie, composed a country and western song, created a TV series, and communed with Maasai warriors, Turkish sultans, and Inti the Ecuadorian Sun God.

For a living (and she always wonders why that's most people's number-one question), she has created 18 books, 3 stage plays, a screenplay, a TV series, 2 iPhone apps, and the A.A. 2.0 program. She can be tracked down at www.pamgrout.com, @PamGrout, and www.facebookcom/pam.grout.fanpage.

NOTES

NOTES

NOTES

NOTES

HAY HOUSE TITLES OF RELATED INTEREST

YOU CAN HEAL YOUR LIFE, the movie,
starring Louise Hay & Friends
(available as a 1-DVD program, an expanded 2-DVD set, and an online streaming video)
Learn more at www.hayhouse.com/louise-movie

THE SHIFT, the movie,
starring Dr. Wayne W. Dyer
(available as a 1-DVD program, an expanded 2-DVD set, and an online streaming video)
Learn more at www.hayhouse.com/the-shift-movie

All of the above may be ordered at www.hayhouse.co.uk

HAY HOUSE

Look within

Join the conversation about latest products,
events, exclusive offers and more.

f   Hay House UK

🐦   @HayHouseUK

📷   @hayhouseuk

💜   healyourlife.com

We'd love to hear from you!